TEACHING STUDENTS TO DIG DEEPER

What does it really mean for students to be college and career ready? In this new edition of *Teaching Students to Dig Deeper*, Ben Johnson identifies the ten attributes students need for success, according to key research, the College Board, the ACT, and rigorous state standards. In order to thrive beyond high school, students must become…

- ◆ Analytical thinkers
- ◆ Critical thinkers
- ◆ Problem solvers
- ◆ Inquisitive
- ◆ Opportunistic
- ◆ Flexible
- ◆ Open-minded
- ◆ Teachable
- ◆ Risk-takers
- ◆ Expressive

But how? Johnson offers the answers, providing practical strategies and techniques for making the ten attributes come alive in the classroom, no matter what grade level or subject area you teach. With the book's strategies and tools, you will be inspired, armed, and ready to help all of your students think on a deeper level and expand their learning.

Ben Johnson is an educational leader and change agent with a mission to help students learn more by increasing teacher and administrator effectiveness. As Assistant Superintendent, he turned around a school district from near unacceptable to recognized in three years. He has mentored and coached multitudes of school instructional leaders to increase student learning throughout the state of Texas.

Also Available from Routledge Eye On Education

(www.routledge.com/eyeoneducation)

Rigor and Assessment in the Classroom
Barbara R. Blackburn

Rigor Is Not a Four-Letter Word, 2nd Edition
Barbara R. Blackburn

**Rigor in Your Classroom:
A Toolkit for Teachers**
Barbara R. Blackburn

**The Genius Hour Guidebook:
Fostering Passion, Wonder, and Inquiry in the Classroom**
Denise Krebs and Gallit Zvi

STEM by Design: Strategies and Activities for Grades 4-8
Anne Jolly

DIY Project Based Learning for Math and Science
Heather Wolpert-Gawron

DIY Project Based Learning for ELA and History
Heather Wolpert-Gawron

**Moving from What to What If? Teaching Critical Thinking with Authentic
Inquiry and Assessments**
John Barell

**Let's Get Real: Exploring Race, Class, and Gender Identities
in the Classroom**
Martha Caldwell and Oman Frame

**Passionate Learners: How to Engage and Empower Your Students,
2nd Edition**
Pernille Ripp

Passionate Readers: The Art of Reaching and Engaging Every Child
Pernille Ripp

Teaching Students to Dig Deeper

Ten Essential Skills for College and Career Readiness

Second Edition

Ben Johnson

Routledge
Taylor & Francis Group

NEW YORK AND LONDON

Second edition published 2018
by Routledge
711 Third Avenue, New York, NY 10017

and by Routledge
2 Park Square, Milton Park, Abingdon, Oxon, OX14 4RN

Routledge is an imprint of the Taylor & Francis Group, an informa business

First edition published by Routledge 2013

Library of Congress Cataloging-in-Publication Data
Names: Johnson, Ben (Ben Stewart), 1960- author.
Title: Teaching students to dig deeper: ten essential skills for college
and career readiness / by Ben Johnson.
Description: Second edition. | New York : Routledge, [2017] |
Includes bibliographical references.
Identifiers: LCCN 2017019489| ISBN 9781138055834 (hk) |
ISBN 9781138055858 (pbk) | ISBN 9781315165653 (ebk)
Subjects: LCSH: Thought and thinking–Study and teaching–United States. |
Education–Standards–United States. | College preparation
programs–United States.
Classification: LCC LB1590.3 .J645 2017 | DDC 370.15/2–dc23
LC record available at https://lccn.loc.gov/2017019489

ISBN: 978-1-138-05583-4 (hbk)
ISBN: 978-1-138-05585-8 (pbk)
ISBN: 978-1-315-16565-3 (ebk)

Typeset in Palatino
by Deanta Global Publishing Services, Chennai, India

MEET THE AUTHOR

Ben Johnson loves working with teachers, students, and parents in his calling as an educator. He has 32 years of experience in helping students and teachers to increase learning capacity. He has a doctoral degree from the University of Phoenix in Education Leadership, and Curriculum and Instruction. During his career, Ben Johnson has carried such auspicious titles as Teacher, Campus Administrator, District Administrator, University Program Manager, and Private Consultant. Like many educators, he has also adopted many other titles in "off times" in order to provide for his family. He began his career as a Spanish teacher and has never forgotten the important lessons he learned there:

- The mouth is connected to the brain, and if the mouth is moving correctly the brain is also. Students cannot be expected to remember something they cannot pronounce.
- Students must have a reason to learn the language (or anything).
- The rule of three—students need at least three opportunities to learn for each concept.
- The basis of all learning is Comprehensible Input.

Ben is a strong proponent of Professional Learning Communities in schools. He is especially interested in helping teachers align their instruction to natural workings of the brain. Effective questioning, formative assessments, and technology are tools that help him do this. What little extra time that Ben has he spends with his family in Tyler, Texas and dotes on his children and grandchildren. He stays active in his church and tries to keep physically fit in the swimming pool. Ben also writes a monthly blog for Edutopia.org.

CONTENTS

PREFACE

What's New in the Second Edition

This edition has been enhanced by enlarging the scope of the college- and career-readiness concept to include a broader national and international view of career readiness and college readiness. Whereas the first edition focused almost entirely on the Common Core, this edition uses more widely accepted standards from individual states, National Association of Colleges and Employers (NACE), American College Testing (ACT), Advancement Via Individual Determination (AVID), Association for Career and Technology Educators (ACTE), American School Counselor Association (ASCA), College and Career Competency Framework (CCCF), Texas Coordinating Board (TCB), and Career Readiness Partner Council (CRPC). Educators reading this book will find it easier to integrate the ten traits into their instructions due to a more uniform approach for applying the college- and career-readiness traits; each chapter has three strategies and each strategy has three technique ideas for helping students acquire the traits discussed. The explanations of the strategies and techniques have been revised and updated to better coordinate with the chapters and focus on developing the specific college- and career-readiness trait. Additionally, the references in each chapter have been reviewed and updated as necessary.

This enhanced edition provides you with powerful tools to prepare your students for what awaits them outside your classroom, but be patient with your students because they may not be accustomed to being pushed and stretched mentally. Most of all, I hope you enjoy reading this new edition as much as I enjoyed writing it.

INTRODUCTION

Students are being pushed to go to college from the first day they enter kindergarten. Teachers struggling to provide relevance to what they are teaching frequently admonish students, "You will need to know this when you go to college!" Even worse, schools and school districts are "graded" by how many students are evaluated as "college-ready." But no one puts such pressure on students and teachers to be career-ready, even though they pay it lip service by tagging it onto their efforts, calling it "college- and career-ready."

Dr. Hope Clark, from American College Testing (ACT), explains that the definition of college readiness is pretty well agreed upon by all: "College readiness is defined by 'the level of achievement a student needs to be ready to enroll and succeed—without remediation—in credit-bearing first-year postsecondary courses."

Dr. Clark goes on to say that career readiness does not have such a clean, well-regarded definition. Part of the problem is that being career-ready is hard to pin down because in today's society it is common for individuals to have multiple careers. She did provide a general career readiness definition that takes this into account: "the level of 'foundational skills' and individual needs for success in a career pathway or career cluster, coupled with the level of 'career planning skills' needed to advance within a career path or transition to other career paths" (2015):[1] "Work readiness is defined as the level of 'foundational skills' and individual needs to be minimally qualified for a specific occupation/job as determined through an occupational profile or job analysis."

While each state has its own definition of what it considers to be "college-ready and career-ready" (CCR), the sad fact of the matter is that for all the hype about CCR, less than a third of the students graduating from high schools across the nation are able to meet even the minimum state college-readiness standards (Combs et al., 2010).

I have spoken with many college students and they confirm this data. For example, I spoke to Audry Posky, who is the life guard at the swimming pool where I swim every morning (mentioned here with her permission). I discovered that she was a second-year nursing student at the local college. I asked

1

smaller the business, the more crucial any hire is. Be flexible on background requirements, but continue to be stringent on personality traits.

Every nation or state, the College Board, and ACT can tell you the college- and career-readiness success predictors on their tests because they can measure all the content knowledge and skills that need to be acquired and mastered before entering the workforce or college, but little has been done to measure resiliency, persistence, or teach-ability. This book will focus on those and other "difficult to measure" soft skills that, almost uniformly, every employer and college professor wishes incoming employees and freshman possessed.[6] I have distilled out of Dr. Conley's work ten distinct qualities identifying college-ready and career-ready students, and I have taken the liberty of labeling them in terms of student traits (see Figure i). I also did a comparison of the major CCR standards with these ten traits (see Figure ii). As you can see, the *Teaching Students to Dig Deeper* traits include all of the CCR Standards from the higher-education and the business perspectives. Notice the strong correlation between strictly college-prep entities and career entities.

Students who are college and career ready possess the following attributes. Our task, more than ever before, is to help them, our students, acquire these essential skills.

In this book, you will find a treasure trove of specific strategies for promoting the growth and development of these college-/career-readiness traits.

Figure ii   College and Career Readiness Traits

Analytic thinkers
- They think about the parts and pieces of the whole.

Critical thinkers
- They think about effectiveness and validity of arguments.

Problem solvers
- They synthesize disparate parts to create a solution.

Inquisitive
- They have the curiosity enough to research and discover independently.

Opportunistic
- They take advantage of learning opportunities and prefer to learn now rather than later.

Flexible
- They have the ability and desire to cope with frustration and ambiguity and work with others on a team or collaboration.

Open-minded
- They are willing to accept critical feedback from peers and supervisors or instructors.

Teachable
- They are willing to adjust their ideas based on feedback.

Risk-takers
- In seeking success, they are open to possible failure and ready to learn from both.

Expressive
- They are able to communicate both in writing and orally.

Figure iii Comparison of TSDD to CCR National Standards

Teaching Students to Dig Deeper (TSDD) compared to College Readiness Standards from National and State Organizations

TSDD-Traits of College and Career Ready Students	NACE	ACT	AVID	ACTE	ASCA	CCCF	TEXAS TCB	CRPC
1. Analytic thinkers (they think about the parts and pieces of the whole)		✓	✓	✓	✓		✓	
2. Critical thinkers (they think about effectiveness and validity of arguments)	✓	✓	✓	✓	✓	✓	✓	✓
3. Problem solvers (they synthesize disparate parts to create a solution)	✓	✓	✓	✓	✓	✓	✓	✓
4. Inquisitive (they have the curiosity enough to research and discover independently)		✓	✓			✓	✓	
5. Opportunistic (they take advantage of learning opportunities and prefer to learn now rather than later)		✓	✓	✓	✓	✓	✓	
6. Flexible (they have the ability and desire to cope with frustration and ambiguity and work with others on a team or collaboration)	✓	✓	✓	✓	✓	✓	✓	✓
7. Open-minded (they are willing to accept critical feedback from peers and supervisors or instructors)		✓	✓		✓		✓	
8. Teachable (they are willing to adjust their ideas based on feedback)		✓	✓		✓	✓	✓	
9. Risk-takers (in seeking success, they are open to possible failure and ready to learn from both)		✓	✓		✓	✓		
10. Expressive (they are able to communicate both in writing and orally)	✓	✓	✓		✓	✓	✓	✓

National Association of Colleges and Employers (NACE), American College Testing (ACT), Advancement Via Individual Determination (AVID), Association for Career and Technology Educators (ACTE), American School Counselor Association (ASCA), College and Career Competency Framework (CCCF), Texas Coordinating Board (TCB), and Career Readiness Partner Council (CRPC).

Each chapter is composed of two parts: the "why," or theoretical part based on research, and the "how" part, based on best practices. I encourage you also to read these chapters critically, or, as Dr. Michael Schmoker, author of *Results Now* and *Focus*, suggests, "with pen in hand." Write all over the margins. Note down your doubts, questions, observations, and disagreements. Ultimately, what you get out of this book is not what I have to say, but what you think about what I have to say, and that makes all the difference in what you learn.

Enjoy.

Notes

1 Clark, H. (February, 2015). Building a Common Language for Career Readiness and Success: A Foundation Competency Framework for Employers and Educators. ACT Working Papers Series. Retrieved January 23rd, 2017 from https://www.act.org/content/dam/act/unsecured/documents/WP-2015-02-Building-a-Common-Language-for-Career-Readiness-and-Success.pdf.

2   Texas College and Career Readiness Standards (CCRS), printed in 2009, talks mainly about college readiness, stating that, "… over 80% of 21st century jobs will require some post-secondary education." The Texas Higher Education Coordinating Board (THECB ... not The College Board) implies that if the students are ready for college, they are ready for the workforce (see pp. iv–v).

3   While the cost to join NACE is a bit prohibitive for individuals, they do provide excellent post-college career-readiness materials, lesson plans, articles, and guides free of charge at http://www.naceweb.org/career-readiness/competencies/sample-materials/.

4   College & Career Competency Framework, by Research Collaboration, provides a complete teaching program for each of the 26 competencies they list. They also provide three handy resources for parents to help them prepare their teens for college and career. http://www.cccframework.org/resources.html.

5   You can find this interesting article at https:// http://onforb.es/16hjFfc.

6   In the Standards for Success study produced by Dr. Conley (2003), over 400 college and university professors were queried concerning the knowledge and skills necessary to be successful in their particular coursework. EPIC has added to this original study thousands of surveys from college professors.

References

Association for Career and Technical Education—ACTE—Academic Skills, Employability Skills, Technical Skills (Job Specific).

ATD—Association for Talent Development. Retrieved January 23rd, 2017 from https://www.td.org/Publications/Magazines/TD/TD-Archive/2013/01/Training-and-Development-Competencies-Redefined.

Barber, J. (2016). Illustrating Career Readiness Competencies: Part II, Inside Higher Ed. Retrieved January 23rd, 2017 from https://www.insidehigh-ered.com/advice/2016/11/14/how-phd-students-can-demonstrate-employers-they-are-career-ready-essay.

Camara, W. (2013). Defining and Measuring College and Career Readiness: A Validation Framework. *Educational Measurement: Issues & Practice*, *32*(4), 16–27. doi:10.1111/emip.12016.

Caron, S. W. (2011). Tomorrow's Workforce: What Students Need. *Education World*. Retrieved January 23rd, 2017 from http://www.educationworld.com/a_admin/tomorrows-workforce-what-students-need.shtml.

Clark, H. (2015). Building a Common Language for Career Readiness and Success: A Foundation Competency Framework for Employers and Educators. *ACT Working Papers Series*. Retrieved January 23rd, 2017 from https://www.act.org/content/dam/act/unsecured/documents/WP-2015-02-Building-a-Common-Language-for-Career-Readiness-and-Success.pdf.

College and Career Competency Framework: Research Collaboration www.cccframework.org.

Maxwell, N. (2006). *The Working Life: The Labor Market for Workers in Low-skilled Jobs.* Kalamazoo, Michigan: W.E. Upjohn Institute for Employment Research. Retrieved January 23rd, 2017 from https://books.google.com/books?id=3cZO0cTOOTMC&pg=PA181&dq=o%27neil,+harold+f.&hl=en&sa=X&ved=0ahUKEwjxi6qG2dbRAhVM4GMKHdWXDGY4ChDoAQhKMAg#v=onepage&q=o'neil%2C%20harold%20f.&f=false.

National Association of Colleges and Employers (NACE). www.naceweb.org/knowledge/career-readiness-competencies.aspxf.

O'Neil, H. (2014). *Workforce Readiness: Competencies and Assessments.* New York, New York: Psychology Press. Retrieved January 22nd, 2017 from https://books.google.com/books?hl=en&lr=&id=9mgAAwAAQBAJ&oi=fnd&pg=PP1&dq=vocational+readiness+standards&ots=l3MmqCo383&sig=rosnVTvrj2hB13T1uxEAN58PffM#v=onepage&q=vocational%20readiness%20standards&f=false.

SCANS—Secretary's Commission on Achieving Necessary Skills—US Department of Labor. (1999). Retrieved March 16th, 2017 from https://wdr.doleta.gov/opr/fulltext/document.cfm?docn=6140.

Sundheim, K. (2013). *Fifteen Traits of an Ideal Employee. Forbes.* Retrieved March 17th, 2017 from https:// http://onforb.es/16hjFfc.

Texas Higher Education Coordinating Board. (2009). *Texas College and Career Readiness Standards.* Austin, Tx: University Printing Services University of Texas at Austin.

Section I

Creating Thinkers

Introduction to Analytical Thinking, Critical Thinking, and Problem Solving

Analytical thinking and critical thinking are often lumped together with that other Higher-Order Thinking Skill (HOTS) called problem solving. In fact, in most literature, authors, researchers, and education gurus use analytical thinking, critical thinking, and problem solving as interchangeable terms that simply indicate "deeper" thinking. Part of the reason that educators confuse these terms is that these cognitive skills often appear to use some of the same thinking techniques. In actuality, what really occurs is that what looks on the surface like pure problem solving is actually a combination of skills being brought to bear on the problem. To be able to solve a problem, the thinker must think analytically, critically, and creatively, and not necessarily in that order. I need to make sure we are all on the same page, because if we want students to effectively use these cognitive skills on the job or in college, we need to be crystal clear as to what they really are, so we can provide learning opportunities that promote them. To this end, I would like to help you differentiate these three thinking skills in the first three chapters.

Let's start with the basics. Analytical thinking and critical thinking are not the same thing. To clarify the difference between these words, let's look at their etymology (study of word meaning). According to the dictionary, "analyze" means to break apart into essential elements. The opposite of analyze is synthesize, or put together. "Criticize" means to evaluate or make a judgment regarding value, merits, or faults. The opposite of criticize in one sense would be praise, or in another sense, the absence of judgment. Simply looking at the two definitions, it is obvious that two different skill sets are required. So why are they often lumped together? Perhaps we use the words as synonyms because they both require "hard" thinking or significant mental effort. I think we perpetuate fuzzy thinking when we are not clear to our students about what each type of thinking really is.

Figure I.1   Rubik's Question (Gideon Johnson, 2012)

To graphically illustrate the difference between analytical thinking and critical thinking, I have included Figure I.1 (drawn by my son Gideon Johnson when he was a high school student). If you look at it carefully, you will see more than a series of Rubik's cubes placed in the form of a question mark. You will see that the cubes may appear to be random configurations of the cube except for the last one. In looking more closely, you will see that they are placed in a sequential pattern from most disorganized to most organized. Not only that, but if you pull out your own Rubik's cube and mimic the pattern, you will see something amazing. You will solve the riddle of the cube. That is pure analytical thinking at its best. There was no need for judgment when my son drew this image on the computer. OK, he did have to choose (be critical about) which design was best and what to include in the design, but the demonstration of how he solves the cube was pure analysis.

Benjamin Bloom (1956) made the specific distinction between analytical thinking (analysis) and critical thinking (evaluation), stating that the two skills differ in cognitive difficulty by two orders of magnitude (Lorin Anderson, in her revision of *Bloom's Taxonomy of the Cognitive Domain*, changed it so they differ by only one [Pohl, 1999]). So, according to Bloom, thinking critically is much more difficult than thinking analytically. The reason for this has already been discussed: in order to think critically, one must understand what one is criticizing. The way to understand something is to look at it analytically: break it down into parts, figure out how it works, classify it, etc. Once that is done, then critical thinking can be undertaken: asking why it works, looking for reasons, finding limits and exceptions, judging value, discovering errors, etc.

To clearly express the differences among these three thinking skills, I would like to share another example. Analytical thinking is what my son applied to the electric mixer to find out how it worked. He took it apart, piece-by-piece. He saw how the pieces fit together and how each part interacted with the other parts. With this analytic knowledge, he was able then to re-create the inner workings of the mixer on a computer drafting program and send his drawings to a 3D printer to sculpt a plastic prototype. In the analysis process, he discovered a design flaw in the construction of the mixer; when a plastic gear is used on a metal gear, the metal gear wins every time. As it turned out, the plastic gears that spin the beaters had worn down to the point that they allowed the motor to run freely without engaging the beaters at all, which makes mixing by electric mixer more laborious than simply using a spoon (oh, and that reminds me of the story of the fellow who bought a chainsaw … I digress[1]). My son used critical thinking when he determined that the mixer could not be fixed easily and recommended purchasing a new one. Problem solved!

The following three chapters discuss in detail analytical thinking, critical thinking, and problem solving as college- and career-readiness attributes. Each chapter describes the research and then provides strategies and techniques for teachers to help students acquire these attributes and to dig deeper.

Note

1 A backwoodsman went to a home improvement store and purchased a chainsaw to replace an old worn-out saw. After a month, the backwoodsman returned the saw to the store, "It doesn't work worth a darn! I could hardly cut half the wood I normally do." The salesman looking at the chainsaw and seeing nothing wrong, pulls the cord. The chainsaw starts easily with a roar. The backwoodsman jumps back, "Tarnation, what's all that racket? When I used it to saw, it was plumb silent!"

References

Bloom, B. S. (1956). *Taxonomy of Educational Objectives, Handbook I: The Cognitive Domain*. New York, NY: David McKay Co. Inc.

Pohl, M. (2000). *Learning to Think, Thinking to Learn: Models and Strategies to Develop a Classroom Culture of Thinking*. Cheltenham, Australia: Hawker Brownlow.

Analytical Thinkers

Analytical Thinking: Thinking about the Parts and Pieces

Why Do Students Need to Be Analytical Thinkers?

Who was an analytical thinker? Hmm. Wasn't Aristotle the first to be classified as an analytic thinker? Aristotle, who lived from 384 to 322 B.C.E., was one of Plato's students. Later he tutored Alexander the Great. Aristotle took his place in Athens as a great educator in his own school, called the Lyceum. He was a keen observer, which is the first prerequisite of being analytical. After careful observations, he described the world he saw and broke it down into all of its pieces. In his writings, he describes his observations of multitudes of subjects. For example, he describes humans as having form and substance, and says that in order to be human, one must have both. This sounds pretty reasonable, but we know now that some of his observations were wrong. For example, his observations led him to believe that Earth was at the center of the universe and that all celestial objects revolved around it. This reminds me of the story by John Godfrey Saxe of blind men describing the elephant according to the parts they were touching.[1] Each accurately described his own experience but entirely missed the target on what the whole elephant looked like.

Seymour Papert (1980), celebrated MIT professor, shared that his analytical thinking as a youth was greatly strengthened by the concept of gears, cogs, and wheels. Their interplay fascinated him, so he tried to figure out how moving one gear might affect the entire system and how all the gears and cogs changed speeds, torque, and directions. From his fascination with gears and cogs, Dr. Papert created a computer language (LOGO) to help students increase their analytical thinking by controlling the path of an electronic "turtle."[2]

In the movie *I.Q.* (1994), the hero, Ed Walters, played by Tim Robbins, sailed through the first part of an "intelligence" test, which consisted of patterns of wooden blocks, complex interconnecting pieces, and a puzzle box. But he needed help from Albert Einstein, played by Walter Matthau, when it came to the actual "content" or principles of physics. As the story goes, Ed Walters was good at puzzles because he was an auto mechanic, accustomed to the intense analytical thinking involved with taking apart and putting back together transmissions.

Malcom Gladwell says that Bill Joy, the brilliant mind behind Unix, Java, and Sun Microsystems, is a success story because of the "10,000-hour rule"[3] and because he was born in the right place at the right time, which for the computer industry was 1953–1955. He is a computer programmer extraordinaire and an analytical thinker who can think in terms of procedures, heuristics, and algorithms. For him, coding computers is as easy as riding a bicycle. His analytical thinking includes two types of knowledge: he must know the capacity and operation of the computer and he must be fluent in the coding language that tells the computer what to do and how to do it.

All of those examples show what analytical thinking is and describe its limitations. Analytic thinkers are investigators, organizers, categorizers, labelers, and specifiers, but they only do these things within what they have experienced. For the most part, analysis is restricted to what can be seen or touched, manipulated or observed. Analytical thinkers use analytic strategies and analytic techniques to understand how things work, how they fit together, and how they relate to other things. Analytical thinkers use strategies such as logic to determine how things operate. Another strategy they use is to think in terms of systems and interactions among systems. To support their chosen or preferred strategy, analytical thinkers use analytical thinking techniques such as abstraction, Boolean logic (AND, OR, NOT OR, XOR, IF THEN), and identifying similarities and differences. We will be discussing these strategies and their supporting techniques for analytical thinking in the second half of this chapter.

Perhaps the best way to express the essence of analytic thinking is to use an example from one of the best thinkers around, Shel Silverstein. I love reading his poems because he takes common, self-evident statements, concepts, and household articles and turns them on their heads through his literal interpretations. Reading his work makes a person think, laugh, and then think some more. Using analytical thinking, Silverstein vividly recounts in verse the story of Melinda Mae who solved her whale problem one bite at a time. The heart of analytic thinking is taking a big task and breaking it down into bite-sized pieces, then looking at all the parts and making sense of them, one piece at a time. Sometimes it takes a bit of effort to find all the parts or identify that something is a unique part, but once the parts are all identified, then the thinker can figure them out. He can identify the purpose, methods, and interactions of each part until he knows how the whole thing works. This can be quite laborious if there are many parts. Vincent Ruggiero (2009) recounts the history of Walter Chrysler, who, as a railroad mechanic, purchased a Pierce Arrow automobile with the sole purpose of taking it apart, piece-by-piece, to discover how it worked and identify any possible ways to improve on it. We all know the rest of the story. Today we would call what he did reverse engineering, which is a common industrial practice, the movie *Paycheck* (2003) with Ben Affleck and Uma Thurman being a perfect futuristic example of this. Affleck plays Michael Jennings, an expert in reverse engineering who hires himself out to reverse engineer a competitor's holographic technology. The movie starts by showing Jennings not only creating a working model that was slightly different to satisfy the patent office, but also making it even better than the original model. (So as to not leave you hanging if you haven't seen the movie, the plot shows Jennings in trouble after his last job and trying to figure out obscure clues of the future that he left for himself. It's a good movie.)

The Importance of Analytic Strategies and Techniques

Jigsaw puzzles are full of pieces that require us to think analytically in order to assemble them. We have all tried to solve jigsaw puzzles and have our own preferred methods. I think everyone would agree that the hardest way to solve a jigsaw puzzle is to try to connect one piece to another piece by simply testing each piece until you find the one that fits (this is what a computer would do—called a Boolean search). This strategy might work on a junior puzzle with ten pieces, but it would take years to complete a puzzle with a thousand pieces. Good jigsaw puzzlers use a strategy to speed up the process and guide their techniques. They have a strategy or mindset for looking at the solution to the whole problem. By adhering to this way of thinking, they can finish the puzzle in the shortest amount of time. For example, some puzzlers focus more on the colors rather than the shapes of the pieces and organize the pieces in piles of similar colors, thus increasing the likelihood of finding the right matches with fewer attempts. Then they look for the shapes. Other puzzlers focus on the big picture and form the frame of the entire puzzle first, then they work inward. Most of us do both.[4] The jigsaw examples demonstrate that good analytical thinkers always have a guiding strategy and several supporting techniques at their beck and call to help them increase understanding and make the right connections, jigsaw-like.

Analytical Thinking and College and Career Readiness

Analytic thinkers are philosophers, college professors, transmission mechanics, and computer programmers. They reverse engineer, tinker, and solve puzzles by using strategies to guide their thinking and employing techniques as if they were tools. To be truly college- and career-ready requires that students not only acquire the necessary knowledge but also build their analytical thinking muscles in the process of gaining that knowledge. This means that students must be proficient at analyzing (breaking apart) all genres, media, and methods. Students must identify underlying structures, thoughts, and motives. Students must be practiced at applying logical steps in math, and identifying similarities to categorize plants and animals in science. Piecing together the puzzles is only the means to gain understanding, but it is an entirely necessary process in order for learners to understand the world in ways that make sense to them, right or wrong.

How to Help Students Become Analytical Readers

The role of the teacher is to show students analytical thinking strategies with their corresponding techniques and then create learning opportunities that require students to use them in order to learn content and gain abilities. The magic of reading is that through the words of others, students don't have to travel to England to learn the deductive skills of Agatha Christie's Hercule Poirot. Through analytic reading, students can travel back in time and look over the shoulder of John Jay, James Madison, and Alexander Hamilton as they write *the Federalist Papers*, or Shakespeare as he pens the poignant messages of *The Tempest*. Through analytic reading, students can envision the future, get into the brain of Albert Einstein, and really understand gravity through the General Theory of Relativity. Analytical thinking is the backbone of all learning. Unfortunately, well-meaning teachers and professors, much like the proverbial tinkerer with the alarm clock, often take a subject and break it down analytically, but forget to put it back together, which makes it essentially useless for the sleeper and the students. Our job is to make sure we lead the students not only to disassemble but also reassemble the concepts and ideas.[5]

The rest of this chapter will help you to learn about effective, best-practice analytical thinking strategies and supporting techniques for each strategy that you can immediately apply in your classroom.

How to Help Students Think Analytically

S T R A T E G Y

Abstract Thinking to Enhance Analytical Thinking

Give teenagers the old piece of wisdom, "A rolling stone gathers no moss." Typical teenage response: "Mick Jagger has moss?" Tell teenagers, "Don't cry over spilt milk." They'll say, "It's only milk, why cry?" Say, "Too many cooks spoil the soup." They'll respond, "I hate soup." Mention, "water under the bridge." They'll say, "Of course there is water under a bridge!" Say, "A tiger's stripes do not change." You'll hear "Duh." Tell teenagers, "Birds of a feather flock together." "Yeah, those grackles downtown are so annoying." There must be millions of them.

A college-ready student can think figuratively, or in other words, can associate abstract ideas with concrete examples. One of the best ways to help students think abstractly is to engage them in the ancient wisdom of metaphors and adages. While not exactly parallel, thinking figuratively through metaphors, analogies, and allusions is a first step toward thinking abstractly. Initially, students' reactions will be like the ones above, but with a little practice, they will be able to arrive at the real meaning of the sayings. Thinking abstractly is useful for understanding the richness of both classic and modern literature. Carroll's *Alice's Adventures in Wonderland*, Dr. Seuss' *Horton Hears a Who*, and Milton's *Paradise Lost* would be incomprehensible without the ability to think abstractly.

The reason that algebra, geometry, and general mathematics challenge students is that they require students to think abstractly. The bane of most students—solving word problems—involves transforming something concrete into abstract symbols and numbers. Most problem-solving techniques require students to step back (figuratively) from the problem at hand (it could be at foot) and state the problem in abstract terms.

In order to help my students improve their abstract thinking and their skill in using the Spanish language, I wrote a *dicho* (a saying) on the board, such as my favorite one, "*En boca cerrada no entra mosca!*"(In a closed mouth, flies don't enter). I asked students to decipher the Spanish and then provide the real meaning. Once we got past the literal interpretations, students were usually able to arrive at approximate meanings. Some *dichos* stumped them at first: "*Al hambriento, no hay pan duro*" (To the hungry, there is no hard bread) or "*En casa del herrero, cuchillo de palo*" (In the house of the blacksmith, a wooden knife).

TECHNIQUE: *Let them struggle*. I found that the key to helping students the most is counterintuitive. Part of me wants to just give them the answer, but in terms of actual learning, the best course of action is to refrain. To let them figure the *dicho* out and only nudge them a bit if they get stuck. So I put on my Socratic robes and asked questions instead. My questions attempt to guide their minds to look at other possible meanings. It is hard for students in the beginning, but with practice, they eventually get the hang of looking at things figuratively. They begin to see the deeper messages in the *dichos* and are able to transfer that skill to see deeper messages in Spanish humor and literature. It was always illuminating and inspiring to watch as students caught the joke or the meaning of a literary passage. Students are smarter than we give them credit sometimes—*El león no es como lo pintan* (the lion is not how it is painted).

TECHNIQUE: *Provide a writing stem*. One of the characteristics of college- and career-ready students is that they can form complete sentences. The students love trying to interpret the *dichos* but they will always want to answer in partial sentences if we let them. We have to make full-sentence answers an expectation in our classroom. To help students be conscious about answering questions in full sentences, we can provide them a stem to begin the sentence:

I think this means…
This relates to…
I believe that…

TECHNIQUE: *Partner chat*. One or two students always want to share their thoughts on the *dichos*. I know others have thoughts too, but they often are embarrassed about sharing their ideas with the whole class. Instead of right away asking for one individual to share his or her thoughts, why not ask the students to share with a partner. Between the two, they choose the best response. Then team up with another partnership and between the four choose the best result. Then ask them to pick one of the partners to present the best response to the *dicho* or problem to the whole group. This last step is crucial because without it, the partners tend to get off task. You can do this in ten to fifteen minutes.

S T R A T E G Y

Logic

Analytical thinking assumes there are reasons and underlying rules that govern the way things are and the way things work. Knowing the rules is half the battle. Being able to correctly apply the rules is the other half. Helping students identify and utilize the governing rules is a way to organize their thinking in a logical fashion.

TECHNIQUE: Syllogisms. Syllogisms are tri-part logical statements that help students analyze conclusions using deductive and inductive methods (there really is no difference between deductive and inductive thinking—they both look at facts and make a guess at the meaning or the conclusion based on those facts). The classic syllogism is "Animals have four legs; a dog has four legs; therefore a dog is an animal." Switching things around a bit by using quantifying terminology to refine the relationships—such as all, some, none, always, etc.—is an easy way to enhance that syllogism and get students to think deeper.

TECHNIQUE: Logical operations, AND, If, Or, NOT Or. Most people do not realize that they use logical operations all the time. A simple Boolean search on Google is a lesson on logical operators. Students can search for (appropriate) topics and see the difference in the results returned by adding AND or NOT OR. Applying these same logical operations to the analysis of text can help students identify the main theme(s) from the text and check the sequencing or logical flow of the argument. Geometric proofs follow logical operations, as do algebraic theories and postulates. In reading Shakespeare, students can map the concepts with *AND, OR, NOT* to understand what is really being stated.

TECHNIQUE: *Program a partner.* Have one partner create movement actions for the other partner to follow, much like the LOGO turtle.[6] This requires that both the designer and the follower think analytically of distance, direction, and speed. And it requires that both students agree on the units of measure for distance, speed, and direction. If the technology is available, LEGO® robotics are perfect tools to teach logic. For older students, blindfolding the follower forces both students to think about navigating the classroom full of obstacles and the importance of being precise in giving instructions. I had my Spanish One students do this to learn the commands for giving directions in Spanish.

S T R A T E G Y

Identifying Differences and Similarities

In the seminal book *Classroom Instruction That Works*, Marzano *et al.* (2001) identify that the classroom strategy with the highest effect-size (positive results) based on their meta research was identifying differences and similarities. They are careful to explain that although simply telling students the differences and similarities is a powerful tool, student-directed methods are even more powerful. The gifted educator will make connections to prior knowledge and stack the deck, so to speak, to make it easy for students to analyze the similarities and differences for themselves. What's not the same. Discovering what is wrong or odd with the problem could include determining the differences, which the odd man out, or which element doesn't belong ("One of these things is not like the other, one of these things just doesn't belong ..." remember *Sesame Street?*). Establishing differences and similarities becomes easier when the patterns are clearly identified because what doesn't fit the pattern will seem to shine as if written in neon lights. For example, after reading a selection, once the title, purpose, resources, activities, and consequences have been identified, a valid analytical question is, "What's missing?" Many times additional meaning can be derived as much by what is not stated as by what is. Always keep in mind that learning transfers from one concept to the concept that is being learned if the student is able to recognize similarities or differences in both. For example, being able to ride a bike transfers to being able to ride a motorcycle. Though the experience is fundamentally different, the basic skills necessary are nearly identical.

TECHNIQUE: *Methods of classification—genus, phylum, species.* My daughter loved the game of twenty-one questions, and for Christmas one year, we gave her a computerized version. It consists of a plastic ball that fits in your hand and that plays the game with you by asking you to respond yes or no to a series of questions printed on a small, liquid-crystal screen. Amazingly, every time I played with it, this little device always arrived at the thing that I had chosen. I had to work hard to guess something that it would not figure out. It is almost spooky … unless you understand the principle behind the game. Experts at twenty-one questions (usually eight to twelve years old) will tell you that the way to win the game is to refine the target sample with questions that classify the object as part of a genus, then a phylum, and then a species. Once it is at that level, it is simple to identify the species. There are multitudes of ways to help students categorize, including grouping charts and tables, mind maps, and Venn diagrams. Of particular usefulness is computer software that helps students easily connect the dots. This software includes the Microsoft Office Suite®, FreeMind, Inspiration, Prezi, and HyperStudio®. In Excel and Word, students can create tables, graphs, and charts showing categories and similarities and differences. In PowerPoint®, students can present and describe their discoveries of similarities or differences. FreeMind and Inspiration are programs that help students intuitively organize information in mind maps, flowcharts, and outlines. Prezi is an intriguing presentation tool that allows students to present their topic at the macro level and describe similarities and differences by literally drilling down, magnifying the picture to reveal the connections. HyperStudio is a rich, open-ended multimedia presentation/ creation tool that uses stacks to contain content. As the name suggests, hyper connections are made among the stacks to allow students to create complex interconnections that do not have to be sequential, as in PowerPoint®.

TECHNIQUE: *Identifying patterns—textual CSI.* As already discussed, jigsaw puzzles are fun because we have to identify patterns that match. Finding the next piece to a pattern is a mainstay of intelligence tests and cognition exercises. In the classroom, patterns can be found in the styles of different writing genres. Present students with several different genres of text and have them analyze the technical, connotative, or figurative interpretations of words and phrases in each. Students will then analyze the structure of the sentences and paragraphs. Finally, students will identify the points of view and the intended audience of the text. The task for students will be to identify the genre[7] of the text according to purpose: narrative: sequence of events; procedural: how to; expository: explanation; hortatory (persuasive): get someone to do something; and descriptive: list characteristics. Then students can identify the text type.[8] Perhaps the easiest text type to identify because of its obvious patterns is poetry. The five-paragraph essay follows a different pattern than the newspaper article, which follows a different pattern than the one used by an epitaph.

TECHNIQUE: Frames for writing. Marzano *et al.* (2001), in *Classroom Instruction That Works*, identifies a writing technique used to analyze certain genres and types of literature (pp. 35–42). He shares multiple types of frames that students can use to analyze corresponding literature. Marzano includes a frame for narratives, a frame for expository writing called the "Topic-Restriction-Illustration" frame, a definitions frame, an argumentation frame, a problem/solution frame, and a conversation frame. The frames serve as guides and templates for students to systematically identify the structure and characteristics of certain texts.

Notes

1   You remember the story. Six blind men encountered an elephant for the first time. Each described what the elephant must look like according to what part of the elephant he was touching: Tusk—spear, leg—trunk of a tree, nose—snake, etc. (See Saxe, G. [1873]. *The Poems of John Godfrey Saxe, Complete Edition*. Boston, MA: James R. Osgood and Company.)
2   Seymour Papert wrote a book called *Mindstorms* and created a simple electronic robot. In 1998 the LEGO™ company based its stand-alone robotics on the concepts in Papert's book and today students across the nation compete using the LEGO Mindstorms™ robot kits. The FIRST Robotics competition held annually challenges students to build a robot to perform certain tasks, interact with other robots automatically, and be remote controlled by student drivers. (See http://hackeducation.com/2015/04/10/mindstorms for a fascinating history of LOGO and LEGO.)
3   Malcolm Gladwell's book, *Outliers*, describes how people become successful. The 10,000-hour rule is what he discovered was the threshold of time that needed to be invested in practice for someone to become an expert or exceptional in their chosen venue. Gladwell illustrates this by explaining that great athletes, scientists, computer programmers, and even musicians (like the Beatles) reached this threshold, which allowed them to become superstars.
4   For your information, there is a World Jigsaw Puzzle Federation. Each year teams from various countries compete for the the title of Jigsaw Puzzle Champions. The championship team from France, Les Bleus, was able to complete a whopping 645.21 pieces per hour. Multiply that by the 24 hours of the competition and you have a total of 15,485.04 pieces completed by a team of four-at-a-time puzzlers. According to its website, 27 countries have teams that compete every October. http://www.worldjigsawpuzzle.org/en/home_en.htm. Here is a

cool time-lapsed video of how a group of puzzlers put together a 5,000-piece puzzle over a period of 14 days. Retrieved from https://www.youtube.com/watch?v=WjCL6DgqGN0.

5 MindEdge (2010). Considering the whole part whole learning model. Retrieved February 29th, 2010 from www.mindedge.com/MindEdge_WPW_WhitePaper.pdf.

6 Seymour Papert, the MIT professor who wrote the book *Mindstorms*, created a computer programming language for children that he called LOGO. This language allowed children to control a small robot with a pen that could be raised or lowered. The robot sort of looked like a turtle, so that is what he called it. The robot actually resembled a modern Roomba™ with a dome and could follow directional commands in the LOGO language and raise and lower a pen to leave a line. Later, Papert transferred the LOGO turtle to a computer screen, allowing more young students to program. The language allowed children to give the turtle directions (right, left, forward, etc.), distances, and draw images on the screen.

7 Genre is one of those words that changes meaning according to whom you are speaking. In literature, this is particularly true because the word is used so often in so many different contexts. For an interesting exploration of its meaning, read David Lee's research, "Genres, Registers, Text Types, Domains and Styles: Clarifying the Concepts and Navigating the Path through the BNC Jungle." Retrieved March 22nd, 2012 from http://llt.msu.edu/vol5num3/ pdf/lee.pdf. For all intents and purposes, and in this document, genre means "category."

8 For a no-frills selection of ideas for concept-mapping types of texts, see the following site. Retrieved March 22nd, 2012 from www.cheney268.com/learning/organizers/TypesText.htm

References

Gladwell, M. (2008). *Outliers: The Story of Success*. New York, NY: Little, Brown and Company.

Lee, D. (2012), *Genres, Registers, Text Types, Domains and Styles: Clarifying the Concepts and Navigating the Path through the BNC Jungle.* Retrieved March 22nd, 2012 from http://llt.msu.edu/vol5num3/pdf/lee.pdf.

Maiorana, V. P. (1995). *The Analytical Student: A Whole Learning Study Guide for High School and College Students.* Bloomington, IN: EDINFO Press, Indiana University. Retrieved February 29th, 2012 from http://www.eric.ed.gov/ERICWebPortal/detail?accno=ED374395.

Marzano, R., Pickering, D., and Pollock, J. (2001). *Classroom Instruction That Works: Research-based Strategies for Increasing Student Achievement.* Alexandria, VA: Association for Supervision and Curriculum Development.

Papert, S. (1980). *Mindstorms: Children, Computers, and Powerful Ideas*. New York, NY: Basic Books.

Ruggiero, V. R. (2009). *The Art of Thinking: A Guide to Critical and Creative Thought*. New York, NY: Longman.

Saxe, G. (1873). *The Poems of John Godfrey Saxe, Complete Edition*. Boston, MA: James R. Osgood and Company. Retrieved March 20th, 2012 from http://rack1.ul.cs.cmu.edu/is/saxe/doc.scn?fr=0&rp=http%3A%2F%2Frack1.ul.cs.cmu.edu%2Fis%2Fsaxe%2F&pg=4.

Schepisi, F. (Producer), Schepisi, F. (Director). (1994). *I.Q.* [Motion picture]. USA: Paramount Pictures.

Silverstein, S. (1974). *Where the Sidewalk Ends.* New York, NY: HarperCollins Publishers.

Woo, J. (Producer), Woo, J. (Director). (2003). *Paycheck* [Motion picture]. USA: Dreamworks.

Chapter
2

Critical Thinkers

Critical Thinking: Thinking about
Effectiveness and Validity

Why Do Students Need to Be Critical Thinkers?

Maybe I have watched too many movies and am paranoid, but I believe that people and especially students are far too trusting. "Trust no one!" the hero or heroine is always told, and often it turns out that the person who said not to trust anyone is the one who should not have been trusted.[1] What we hear at schools is a different matter altogether. Students are expected to trust the teacher and the textbook. The system is designed for knowledge to trickle down from those who know to those who do not know. That knowledge is implicitly assumed to be correct, especially by the younger students. I don't believe that I am the only one who has noticed that more and more often students are willing to challenge the teacher (mostly their authority and sometimes their knowledge). It takes a lot of confidence for students to challenge a teacher, and it takes a self-confident teacher to be able to handle these challenges in positive ways. But isn't that what we want? Isn't that what the industry wants? Isn't that what colleges and universities want? We all want students to think critically (evaluate the merits and faults) of what they are learning and not accept blindly what we, the teacher, or textbook says. Later I will discuss the Pandora's box that this will cause to open.

Parents should be asking teachers, "Are my children being prepared to be critical thinkers so that when they get to college, they can stand on their own?" More importantly, parents should be asking, "Does my child know how to be a critical thinker in order to be an effective learner?" To be sure, critical thinking is all about doubting what you read, hear, or see and asking the hard questions, the politically charged questions, and the socially inconvenient questions, but how does that help students learn better? Both parts of this chapter, the Why and the How, will strive to answer that question.

Teachers' Perspectives of Critical Thinking

In this chapter, and frankly in all of the chapters of this book, I want to base your "thinking" on what you might consider to be a selfish concept for teachers: "What's in it for me?" As you read this book, I would like you to momentarily put aside our habitual emphasis on student learning and focus on the benefits of critical thinking for teachers by asking the following question: "How does critical thinking help me, the teacher, in the classroom?"

To begin this conversation, let's look at the pros and cons of critical thinking in the classroom (see Figure 2.1). The "pro" column lists the things that make critical thinking enjoyable and profitable for students. The "con" column contains the typically unmentioned side effects of critical thinking (similar to a warning label on medicinal cures, written in impossibly small type). No particular priority or order was imposed to make the list. In the chapters that follow I would like to persuade you that the benefits described in the

Figure 2.1   How Does Critical Thinking Help Me as a Classroom Teacher?

Critical Thinking Pro	Critical Thinking Con
It makes learning more enjoyable for the learner, more palatable.	It is not quick.
It makes learning memories permanent.	It is frustrating.
It makes learning deeper.	It is overwhelming.
It makes learning naturally more connected.	Nothing is believable.
It develops independent thinkers.	It challenges prior knowledge and assumptions.
It increases content and concept understanding.	It doesn't rest or stop; it is hard to turn off.
It inspires additional learning, it fuels it.	It can be wrong, faulty.
It establishes learner confidence.	It can be misused.
It satisfies a basic human need, to make sense of the world.	It is voracious.
It prepares students for college.	It ruins fantasy.
It honors the efforts students and parents make to come to school.	It does not respect authority or friendship.
It fosters self-confidence.	It promotes argument and debate.
It develops habits of mind.	It develops habits of mind.

"pro" column far outweigh the irritating side effects of the "con" column. As my first evidence, if I figuratively crush all of the items in the "pro" column into a single crucible of thought and grind it up real well, what emerges in the uniform powder is the unique and powerful idea, "Critical thinking helps students be more efficient learners." The idea that critical thinking makes students more effective learners sounds pretty obvious, doesn't it? ("Duh!" some would say.) Common sense dictates that the more we get students to think critically, the better they become at it. Basic, right? Perhaps, but do you know why it works that way, what benefits there are for a teacher, and how teachers can easily bring critical thinking into their lessons? We will look at the "how" in the other half of this chapter, but let's tackle the first two questions now. The answers have to do with the brain and how it works.

The Brain and Critical Thinking

One of my favorite authors has some pretty outlandish things to say about thinking and the brain. Dr. Daniel Willingham (2010), a noted cognitive psychologist, wrote a book that I think every teacher should read and then give to every parent to read. It is appropriately called *Why Students Don't Like School*. Dr. Willingham, right off the bat, tells his readers that they stink at thinking. Or was it think at stinking? Anyway, he says that humans are not good at thinking and so for this reason we have an enormous brain between our ears that helps us find all sorts of ways to avoid thinking. We use memory in terms of routines and habits instead of thinking to get by in everything we do. Habits are formed from memory, not thinking, and we are nothing if not habit-forming creatures. Try going to bed without brushing your teeth, or putting the left sock on first, or folding your arms a different way … you get the idea. We are full of habits—some good, some bad, and some indifferent. Almost every human activity does not require thinking; we do it from memory. However, once in a while, we run across something new and have to think, but more often than not, we think only long enough to remember something similar, and then we don't have to think anymore. That is why experiencing new things is so exhausting—it forces us to think more than we are used to.

Dr. Willingham is a sly one though. He brings up an interesting conundrum. Humans are horrible thinkers, but as it turns out, we actually like thinking even though we are not great at it. Go figure. On one hand, we hate habits and boring routine, but we are awesome at making them, and on the other hand, we are terrible at thinking but we enjoy it.[2] We get a kick out of being stumped and having to figure something out. We love to solve problems, especially other people's problems. We are addicted to puzzles … up to a point. If the puzzle is too hard, it becomes a downer instead of an upper (is that too eightyish?). In other words, we love to be challenged just a bit over our capacity, but if the challenge is too hard, we become frustrated and angry, and the hormone cortisol is released, causing our hippocampus[3] to stop all thought, and we become human vegetables! Or … we simply disengage and do something else.

So why am I telling you all of this, you wonder? I'm getting to a very important point, although I have made a few already—students' brains are designed to depend on memory so they don't have to think; students like thinking, but we can't and shouldn't assume students are good at thinking because they are not (neither are we); and don't make the critical thinking too hard or students will give up. The point I really want to make is that savvy teachers can use their creative skills to design learning activities that give students the opportunity to try critical thinking, push students to the point their brains begins to hurt, and then—quick—give students a test before they forget it. No, no, no—let me finish that last sentence differently: and then ask students to create something with their newfound knowledge to show they really know it. Yes, that is much better!

If you recall, the point of this conversation was to demonstrate that critical thinking makes students more efficient learners. Ok, so now we have arrived at the pinnacle point in the explanation of critical thinking. What Dr. Willingham suggests is that when teachers get students to think, they stimulate memory. This is my favorite quote from Dr. Willingham, "Memory is the residue of thought" (p. 41). After doing all of that hard thinking, what is left over? Memory! So why is that a selfish idea? Because—drum roll please—if students can remember something, we don't have to teach it again! We are done, finished, *terminados*! We can go on to something else. Everybody is happy! Yahoo!

If such a happy ending were easy to achieve, then every teacher would be doing it, right? Some teachers are doing it—students are learning at incredible rates in their classes. But more of us need to be doing it. Critical thinking in classrooms does not usually happen by chance. I should say, productive critical thinking does not happen by chance. It doesn't happen at all without a careful teacher setting the groundwork for it. How do I know that? Think about it. Students are always thinking critically, especially about each other, about cafeteria food, about school in general, and of course, about you. You might call it complaining. Benjamin Bloom would call it evaluating—the hardest cognitive activity to perform. I heard of a teacher who received a devastatingly honest e-mail from a student describing what the teacher was not doing in the classroom, but should be doing, including what specific things the teacher could be doing to fix the problems in the classroom. All this came from a sixth grader! Students know good teaching from bad teaching, but most of the time are too polite, or intimidated, or resigned to their fate, to say anything. The good part of this story is that the teacher, rather than getting all upset—well, after getting all upset—took the message to heart and is now focusing on student learning, getting organized, and dealing with unruly students by channeling their energy into more useful learning activities. But that is another book entirely.

I once walked into a history class with the principal in tow and observed that all the desks were lined up in straight rows and students were at various stages of inattention, ostensibly answering the questions at the end of a chapter. The teacher was not expecting us because this was a surprise walk-through observation. As soon as we walked in, the teacher, who was sitting behind his desk doing something with the computer, stood up, faced the class, and asked a complicated higher-order thinking question. Observing the puzzled looks of the students, the teacher restated the question … with still no response. Changing tactics, the teacher asked a series of questions calculated to guide students to the answer he was seeking. A few light bulbs went on as some students caught the drift of what the teacher was trying to do, but students were still floundering, unable to answer correctly the teacher's simpler questions. The teacher persisted, asking probing question after probing question, to no avail. The principal and I left the classroom.

As we walked down the corridor, I turned to the principal and asked, "What did you see?"

He responded, "The teacher knows how to ask good questions, but the students don't know how to answer them."

"Why couldn't the students answer the questions?" I probed.

The principal looked at me quizzically and replied, "I don't understand it. He is one of our best teachers. Students from his class always score well on state tests."

I nodded in agreement.

"It doesn't appear that the students knew the answers," the principal continued, "and it is obvious that they were not accustomed to answering critical thinking questions."

"So students need to know something in order to answer critical thinking questions," I stated. "And students need practice at answering them," I surmised, while the principal nodded in agreement.

The moral of this story is that just like this history teacher's experience, it would be a waste of time for a teacher to start asking deep critical thinking questions if the students have little content knowledge, and the corollary moral is that for students to be able to answer critical thinking questions, they need to know how to think critically and have some base knowledge about which to think.

How to Help Students Think Critically

S T R A T E G Y

Helping Students Read Critically

Thomas asked, "How do you know that?"
Susan responded, "It says so right here in the textbook?"
Thomas counters, "How does the textbook know that?"
Susan shrugs her shoulders, "… ?"

We have a generation of students who do not know how to read things with a grain of salt (most likely they would wonder what salt had to do with reading). They are trained to automatically trust the textbook, or for that matter, to trust anything that is written. Too often students tell me, "I don't want to figure it out. Just tell me what I need to know." How do we go about fixing this? First of all, we have to get students to read and then get them to read critically. Mem Fox, in her book *Reading Magic* (2001), states that the love of reading has to start young. Parents and teachers have to read at least 1,000 books to children to prepare them to read on their own (p. 17). She also states that if you want your child to stay at home and be close to family, "do not read them stories about the Amazon rain forests." As it turned out, she made the mistake of reading books about France to her young daughter, which prompted her daughter to want to read (know) more about France as she grew older, and guess where her daughter lived when she was twenty, having the time of her life in a new career (p. 128)?

TECHNIQUE: Read with a pen in hand. Dr. Michael Schmoker, in his book *Results Now* (2006), recounts how reading helped Mike Rose transform himself from an educationally uninterested, nearly illiterate student to a successful college professor. Rose went to school in Los Angeles. Until tenth grade, he only went through the motions of learning in school. With his poor literacy, going to school made him feel embarrassed rather than challenged. His tenth-grade teacher finally changed all that by exposing Rose and the other students to a heavy dose of challenging literature, by having students talk about what they read, and by having students write about the issues in the books. Today, Mike Rose is a full professor at UCLA's Graduate School of Education and Information Studies.

Schmoker states emphatically that "Generous amounts of close, purposeful reading, rereading, writing, and talking, as underemphasized as they are in K–12 education, are the essence of authentic literacy" (2006, p. 53). Reading has to be synonymous with thinking. How can you have the one without the other? Reading is an *active* learning method, as opposed to listening, which is *passive*. In order to read, students must be physically engaged—their eye movement tracks words, they turn the pages (or click the mouse or flick the page), they mentally decode symbols to sounds to meaning, they carry a storyline or topic flow in short-term memory, and they arrive at understanding through assimilation of mental images produced by reading the words. With all of that creative learning juice flowing in students' brains while they read, it would be a shame not to take advantage of it. Schmoker shares a simple, helpful strategy: "Read with a pen in hand." As students read, they should make notes in the margins, underline, circle, and highlight.

What? Write in the book? I remember purchasing used books for college that were already highlighted and had notes in them, and they actually helped me study.[4] Didn't they help you? So what is the shelf life of a typical school textbook? Five years? During those five years, do we want the only things written in the textbooks to be graffiti or profanity? Not going to budge? Well, if students can't write in their books, at least they can take notes on a separate piece of paper about what they read. We should teach students to identify concepts while they read and then judge which one is a key concept. Authors tend to do that for students anyway by providing topic headings and subheadings. Then teachers need to help students identify kernels of evidence supporting the key concepts. Using Cornell Notes[5] is a perfect way to do this.

TECHNIQUE: *Cornell Notes.* Let me be perfectly clear here. Cornell Notes, done right, is NOT just a note-taking tool—it is an enhanced thinking process. Do you recall what the residue of thinking is according to Dr. Daniel Willingham? That's right: "The residue of thought is memory" (Willingham, 2010). In simplistic terms, this is how students should use Cornell Notes to read critically: First they write notes about facts and details on the right side of the page as they read. The real learning power comes from taking the time after reading to think about what was read and by asking themselves the hard questions like: "What else do I know about this?" "Why?" "Says who?" "Do I believe it?" The left side of the page should contain these questions along with memory cues, sketches, and subject headings. Finally, at the bottom of the page, students summarize what is most important. Using Cornell Notes the right way can help students read critically, which by the way, helps them remember what they read.

TECHNIQUE: Metacognitive modeling. Critical thinking, like any muscle, improves with practice. It is essential that students not only learn to use critical thinking but also become critical thinkers. The reason students struggle in school, especially in math and science, can be traced directly to their lack of ability to think critically. Metacognitive[6] modeling is simply teachers talking about their own thought processes and how they make sense of what is being learned. When teachers use metacognitive modeling to show students how to think critically, create daily learning experiences in which critical strategies are required, take time to show students how to use multiple critical thinking techniques, and then let students apply those skills, they are preparing their students to be successful in college and careers.

For college- and career-ready students, reading critically is more of a habit of mind than a reading strategy. It should be the default way of reading for every student. The best way for teachers to teach students to read critically is to read critically with them (remember Mem Fox?). You have to model the kind of thinking that needs to happen as you read a story to your students. Share with students how you are thinking and why you are thinking this way in response to a text (this is called metacognition). Now ask students to do the same thing with partners. After you have done this, when you ask students the hard questions (and don't give them the answers), they can answer them. They can tell you if they believe what the text says is true, and they can tell you why they think so. Once you show students how to read critically, it makes your job as a teacher a lot easier. You can expect students to continue to read critically and think critically on every assignment. You should be prepared for them to keep you on your toes; they might start asking why they have to do the assignment in the first place!

S T R A T E G Y

Using Questions to Help Students Think Critically

Most of what we currently consider to be "teaching" depends on a teacher's ability to ask questions of students. Research shows that at least 80 percent of what a teacher does is ask questions (Marzano, *et al.*, p. 113). During typical lessons, teachers ask from 30 to 120 questions per hour or 300 to 400 questions per day (Tienken *et al.*, p. 40).

But even though many questions are asked, the data shows that typical questioning strategies employed in schools today are ineffective at increasing student learning (Zhang *et al.*, 2010, p. 58). Researchers have scratched their heads about this for decades. Some possible reasons for this anomaly are the following: the questions are not at a sufficient level of rigor; the purpose of the questions is off target; the methods of asking the questions are inadequate; and/or the teachers are simply not experienced enough (Rowe, 1974, 1987; Tienken *et al.*, 2009; Albergaria, 2010). As teachers, we need to come to grips with the fact that we really do not know everything. In the same breath, we can safely say that there is no reason to assume that students know nothing. But perhaps before any questions are asked of the students, the most important question to ask is, "What do I as the teacher expect the class to learn from the questioning process? Why ask questions?"

Why Ask Questions?

As I mentioned before, thinking promotes memory, which is what we teachers are all about—we call it learning. We have to get students to think critically about the content, their own thinking, the textbook, their writing, and everything. If we look at the dynamics of any classroom, it doesn't take more than a week for students to figure out who is smart, who is not, and who doesn't care. What's worse, studies (Dossett and Burns, 2000) show that after fourth grade, students know how they are perceived and play their roles accordingly. Using questions to help students think critically can make the classroom environment interesting, lively, and engaging if a few simple techniques are used. The key is to engage as many students as possible. So, we use one of those hook-laden questions that is directed at the entire classroom: "Class, if you could stretch string from here to the moon, how many balls of string would it take?"

The students who know they are not smart are not going to take the bait, and neither will the students who do not care. This leaves the smart kids as the only ones interested in answering, and almost before the question is finished, they have their hands up with an answer, right or wrong. The other two groups of kids are perfectly fine with this routine. Most likely, they are saying to themselves, "Let them answer the questions so I don't have to."

Typically, these are the types of questions that are thrown out to the class as if they were tantalizing treats to be snatched up by all of the eager students. The reality is far different. A teacher may defend this practice because the motivated student who answers will help the whole class learn the answer. That might be true if the whole class were listening, but when the teacher starts pacing the room and stops to ask a question, if students know that the question will be open to the entire class, then most likely two-thirds of the class will not even pay it any attention and will continue doodling or daydreaming. Once again, I ask, do we realize how many general questions we throw to the air in the course of a class period? We would be astounded at the results if we simply assigned a student to tally how many of these questions we actually ask each class period. Old habits are hard to break, but students would love to help you break this one.

When I was an assistant superintendent, I wanted to know what a student actually experiences on a daily basis in our schools. I spent the day as a first grader, a third grader, a fifth grader, a sixth grader, and a ninth grader. I followed these students to all of their classes in a complete school day. During the course of my observations, I saw a disturbing and sad scenario repeated over and over: the same students answered the questions in every class. From this experience, I discovered something so shocking it was hard to believe. Some students actually went through a whole day—maybe even weeks and months for all I know—and never answered a single verbal question!

TECHNIQUE: Ask, wait, then randomly call on students. Let's say we notice this problem and decide something has to change. "Jeffrey," let's name a particular student, "What do John the Baptist and Kermit the Frog have in common?" Several hands slowly recede and all eyes are on Jeffrey. Well, some eyes are on Jeffrey. The rest of the students just breathe sighs of relief that their names were not called. The question asked is not their problem, and neither is the answer; both belong to Jeffrey. Some teachers may say that while Jeffrey is thinking of the answer, the rest of the students are, too. Wouldn't that be nice?

Once again, maybe one-third of the students are thinking about an answer, but the rest are just glad it wasn't them. An easy way to fix this is to appropriately check for understanding: we ask specific questions of specific students! Most of us have been exposed to the questioning strategies researched by Mary Budd Rowe (1974). She proposed that teachers simply ask a question, such as "What do you call it when an insect kills itself?", pause for at least three seconds, and then say a student's name: "Sally." While the teacher waits, all the students should be automatically thinking about an answer because for all they know, they might be chosen next. Only after another child's name is said will they sigh in frustration because they wanted to answer the question, or sigh with relief because they did not know the answer.

Creative teachers accompany this technique with a system to make sure that every child gets to answer questions in a random fashion. Please note that if it is not random that students figure out pretty quickly that if their name is called, they are off the hook for the rest of class. One way to get around that is to make a show of putting the popsicle stick or tongue depressor back in the same cup with all the other students. Students will see that they are not off the hook and may still get called on. What they don't know is that you put the popsicle stick with their name on it in the cup upside-down so you know that you have already called on them once. Even with wait time, only one student is answering questions at one time. How do you engage the other 29 students?

TECHNIQUE: Choral verbal and physical response. The only time it is okay to ask a question of the whole class is when you expect the whole class to answer. Choral answering engages all students, and believe it or not, if you walk around the classroom while students are answering the question all at the same time, you can hear individual answers, and you can tell if they are correct. Interestingly enough, students can tell too, and they self-correct when they realize they are not saying the right answer. The purpose of choral answering is to get all the students to respond—even those reluctant boys. This lowers the affective filter and students feel more comfortable answering the question, whereas if they were the only ones answering the question, they would feel embarrassed. In this way, choral answering builds confidence. A form of choral answering is simply asking students to do something physical, such as touch the right answer, point to the paragraph in their books, stand beneath the poster showing the endoplasmic reticulum, etc. This is called Total Physical Response (TPR) and is an educational version of Simon says. It is a lot of fun for students, as well as for the teacher who thinks of creative ways for students to show that they know the answers—sit on the floor, do the funky chicken, touch the right page with your left elbow, use your chin to point to the word on the wall, etc.

The point of this little sidetrack into effective questioning is to highlight the importance of engaging all students rather than just a few smart ones. Student engagement is so important because it is impossible to get students to think critically in productive ways if they are thinking critically in unproductive ways. Any questions?

TECHNIQUE: Small group consensus. Prepare three question cards that have different levels of questions—easy to hard. Make sure the question is asking one thing—stay away from compound questions. Make a set of these questions for each group of four students. One student will be the question

Figure 2.2 Keeping Track of Roles in Each Group

leader: the person to ask the questions and the one who makes sure all students in the group respond. This student will also try to get a consensus (one answer) from the group. Another will be the presenter of the consensus responses for the group. Another will be the time keeper, while another will take note of decisions or consensus for the reporter to share with the class. (If you create a card that can be placed in the middle of the table with those titles and explanations on each corner [see Figure 2.2], it will save time and allow you to make sure students get opportunities to perform different roles by asking the students to rotate the card.)

Give the students fifteen minutes (set a timer for five minutes per question) to discuss and arrive at consensus for all three questions. Then have the reporter from each group give their answers. Consensus can then be discussed as a class if necessary.

S T R A T E G Y

Using Cognitive Dissonance to Help Students Think Critically

You lower yourself down into the cage, and you tie your hand onto the back of the big brown bull, who snorts with anger and irritation as they cinch the rope tight. You are careful to keep your legs from being smashed between the pen wall and the 1,300-pound jittery bull. You are thankful for the cowboy in the front of the bull who is doing his best to distract it from what you are doing. The three other men who are helping you with the ropes and with getting settled on the bull's back encourage you with the words, "Go get' em, cowboy!" and with pats on the back. Then the gate opens and you hang on for dear life.

You know that you must do two things to make the ride worth it: stay on for eight seconds by responding to and anticipating the rhythms of the bull's movements, and show some style in doing it. The world is in slow motion as you experience the longest eight seconds of your life. The bull heaves its bulk into the air, jumps, twists, and cavorts in every imaginable way to get you and that uncomfortable rope off. You realize that your strength is insignificant compared to the near ton of muscle that is throwing you around like a rag doll. You feel like your arm is going to fall off but you hang on. Seven, eight, the buzzer sounds and you let go of the rope and try to jump free of the angry bull's flailing legs, hooves, and vicious horns. The rodeo clowns get the bull's attention as you dash to safety. After the bull is taken into the pen, you retrieve your hat and your favorite cinching rope from the arena's sandy floor. Only then do you hear the crowd's roar of approval. The thunderous applause with whoops and hollers of appreciation make you stand a little straighter and walk taller. You are just glad to be alive. This time the bull lost.

I took my daughter, Sadie-Belle, to the professional bull riding competition in San Antonio the other day. It was great! This was at the AT&T Center in San Antonio where they play basketball, and it was quite a show. It had been a while since I had watched such an event, and although I have never ridden a bull, I imagine it would be something like I just described. I noticed that some bull-riders wear helmets instead of hats. Most wear padded, protective vests. They all wear gloves and spurs. But it took me a few moments to figure out what the bull-rider's most valuable piece of equipment really is. It is the cinch rope that each rider carefully went back and retrieved from the stadium floor after each ride. As educators, we have a kind of cinch rope, too.

An Educator's Cinch Rope

What is the purpose of the cinch rope? To the uninitiated, the bulls seem like ferocious animals. The opposite is actually normally the case. For the most part, these bulls are docile, calm creatures. I actually saw one of the bulls lie down in the stocks—refusing to get up for the cowboy to ride him. So how do cowboys get a normally sedentary bull to leap in the air? They tie a cinch rope around the bull's chest, and the bull is so uncomfortable that he is anxious to do anything he can to buck the cowboy off for relief. Keep in mind that bulls are trained to do this and are very successful at it. Out of 40 cowboys who rode, only seven were able to stay on their bulls for the full eight seconds.

A teacher's cinch rope is called cognitive dissonance. The term comes from the concept of different sound waves as they collide, creating disharmonic vibrations. It is uncomfortable to listen to such sour notes. Cognitive dissonance is produced when two ideas seem to collide and only one can be right. The educational cinch rope has to be uncomfortable enough for students to do something about it, and just like the bulls, students need to be trained on how to buck you for causing the dissonance. In some cases, the information that students have in their brains is incorrect. For example, if you ask a student what causes the seasons of the year, they will likely tell you that it is because the distance from Earth to the sun changes according to Earth's orbital path. Would you believe me if I told you that the sun is 20 degrees colder in winter than in summer and that causes our seasons? Did I create some dissonance? Neither of the above reasons is true. Are you motivated enough to find out the real answer?[7]

Cognitive dissonance can also be created through the careful gathering and analysis of data to dispel myths, assumptions, and general erroneous beliefs. We have already discussed analytical thinking strategies and tools that help in this regard. Student-led investigations can find answers to questions all students want to know: Does the bread always land butter side down? Do blondes have more fun? Does it take only three licks to get to the center of a Tootsie Roll Pop? How many Skittles can fit in my mouth? Seriously, when students ask the critical thinking questions, like how things work and why things work, then they are ready to learn.

TECHNIQUE: *Cinch rope cognitive dissonance*. Shel Silverstein was a master at cognitive dissonance. He was able to take normal things we see every day and make us think in different ways about them. That is why we love his poetry and his stories. He wrote incongruous poetry and illustrations about topics as odd as eating a whale, putting on socks and pronouncing the word "banana".[8] Data has the capacity to engender cognitive dissonance when critical thinking is applied. Before performing the experiment or data search, students should be required to write what they expect to find. If the data is different, cognitive dissonance ensues. For example, if students in a math class are gathering data about student attitudes and correlating them with right-handedness or left-handedness, this is an opportunity for students not only to graph the data, but also find out what the data is saying and what the implications are, and then ask why the data is the way it is. If students find out that all left-handed people think the same way, the obvious question is, "Why is that so?" "Or is it?"

TECHNIQUE: *Says who?* Every class has a textbook or a text that is designed to make it easy for students to learn the content of the class. In an effort to do this, textbook authors do a lot of summarizing, and they write as if they themselves are the source of information. To introduce students to the idea of supporting arguments with evidence, have them pick apart one of the chapters in their textbook and identify writing that represents opinion versus writing that requires substantiation.

TECHNIQUE: *Critical discussion*. Place students in groups of four or five. Give students a topic of discussion that includes a problem to solve or a conclusion to be reached by consensus. Each student has a name tag or a tent card in front of him/her with a statement written on in like the ones in Figure 2.3 (or something similar). Each statement should be displayed clearly so that other students can easily read what it says.

TECHNIQUE: *Critical brainstorm on literature*. Regular brainstorms are when you identify the main ideas of a text and then brainstorm on all of the related ideas without filtering the ideas. But when an author writes a paragraph, several ideas are generated, but only the best ones get down on paper. Authors critically filter their ideas as they write. In this technique, students learn to think like authors.

In a critical brainstorm, groups of four or five students don't analyze the ideas after all of them are collected, as they would do in regular brainstorms. Instead, they will criticize the ideas as soon as they are suggested. Each idea must refer back to a particular section of the text as evidence to support it. Only ideas that the group decides have a valid point get written

Figure 2.3 Critical Discussion Cue Cards

down as options. Once a list of ideas is created, then the group further winnows the list through discussion until just one idea remains.

Final Comments on Critical Thinking

Necessary Teacher Preparations for Critical Thinking

When you read the fine print on a medicine bottle, it can be kind of scary. In the fine print, they mention the side effects that may occur from taking the medication: "If swelling, itching, or loss of eyesight should occur, stop taking this medication immediately and consult your physician." In most cases, the benefits of taking the drug far outweigh the risk of incurring negative or, heaven forbid, harmful side effects. Implementing critical thinking in the classroom is much like taking a medication. Critical thinking can have side effects in the classroom. Teachers love the critical thinking but also have to deal with those pesky side effects of getting students to think (see Figure 2.4). Teachers have to be prepared to make the necessary adjustments to enable critical thinking as a habit of mind in their students. In order to do so, teachers must accept the fundamental concept that students learn and retain more when they are engaged in critical thinking as expressed in the first part of this critical thinking chapter. In order for students to think critically, teachers have to prepare students with foundational knowledge in the subject area and then train students to be able to ask and answer critical thinking questions.

Figure 2.4 What Critical Thinking Requires of Teachers

It requires
- that teachers assure that students have foundational knowledge.
- a learning-rich environment.
- teachers to be resourceful in leaving breadcrumbs for students to find.

It requires
- teachers to allocate more time up front to learn and discover.
- more time to prepare effective learning experiences.
- teacher patience.
  - a facilitator's discipline to not give the answer.

It requires
- teachers to be examples of critical thinkers.
- teacher self-confidence
  - teachers to be comfortable not knowing the precise outcome of a learning activity.
  - teachers to be comfortable being challenged.
  - teachers to redirect challenges.
- teachers to admit when they do not know.

After teaching students to think for themselves, some teachers may believe that they have created a monster. Students are now challenging what the textbook and teacher have to say, questioning the rules and regulations, making suggestions on how to teach and learn, and constantly asking why, why, why.

The first step in preparing for this barrage of questions is to remember that the teacher does not have to have all the answers; in fact, it is better to play dumb, even if you do have the answer. Make students find it. The trick for minimizing this uncomfortable feeling is to anticipate it and prepare for it. Another thing that will help is to make sure students understand that it is okay to disagree with someone, but it is not okay to be disagreeable about it. In the process of planning for lessons either individually or in professional learning community meetings, think of the critical thinking skills that will be necessary to permanently learn the content of the lesson.

The College Board Standards for College Success™ in English and Mathematics are a tremendous help in this regard. All of the standards that have to do with reasoning, assessing, evaluating, choosing, interpreting, distinguishing, etc. all have elements of critical thinking. For example, The College Board Standards for College Success™ in Mathematics and Statistics clarifies that there are two types of mathematics thinking and that students need both to be successful: deterministic (mathematical), and probablistic (statistical). Both require logical reasoning and pattern recognition so The College Board created curriculum standards that integrate them from middle all the way through high school and label them as Integrated Mathematics level I–VI. As an example of critical thinking that is integrated in their standards, I have extracted a set of performance expectations from the middle school mathematics (or Integrated Mathematics I as The College Board labels it) standard 5: Experimental and Theoretical Probability (see Figure 2.5).

Figure 2.5 *Critical Thinking in Mathematics Standards (The College Board Standards for College Success in Mathematics, p. 10) (Emphasis Added)*

Objective IMI.5.1: Student estimates probabilities in experiments with common objects, including comparing experimental and theoretical probabilities and examining experimental probabilities in the long run. Performance Expectations:	
IMI.5.1.1	Conducts experiments to *estimate the likelihood of a simple event*; compares the experimental probability with an easily identifiable theoretical probability, where the sample space is described by tables or lists of possible outcomes.
IMI.5.1.2	*Describes why* the probability of an event is a number between 0 and 1, inclusive.
IMI.5.1.3	Uses the probabilities of events to compare the likelihoods of events.
IMI.5.1.4	Uses experimental data with graphical or tabular displays to *estimate the probability* of an event for which the theoretical probability is unknown.
IMI.5.1.5	Recognizes that repetitions of an experiment may result in different outcomes, *describes the variation in outcomes* produced in an experiment, and recognizes that with the collection of more data the experimental probability of a particular outcome approaches the theoretical probability.

Once you have determined what you are going to teach, it is time to determine how you will teach it. This is where college- and career-readiness standards can help you. The very first thing you need to do is rough out the lesson and then put yourself in the place of the students. Imagine how students will respond to the learning environment, the learning prompts, and the learning activities. Anticipate student responses to critical thinking and make the necessary adjustments to your lesson. You should know which students to keep away from each other, but more importantly, you should also know which students could inspire in each other new critical thinking skills if they were placed in partnerships or grouped together. As you think "as your students would think," imagine what questions they will have, and steer yourself not to answer their questions directly, but to find ways to reflect the questions back on the students, encouraging them to look in the right locations and seek deeper understanding. Keep the learning responsibility on the shoulders of the students where it belongs.

Please remember that you need to be comfortable with not knowing some things, or at least pretending to not know things. When students are asked to think critically, we may discover that students can come up with the most interesting things, things that we as teachers might not have ever imagined. Critical thinking is one of the most difficult cognitive activities because it requires the use of evaluation, as well as content knowledge gained from analytical thinking. To be effective learners, students must think critically as they read and as they write. Teachers should make sure that students have enough knowledge and understanding to be able to discuss the content of the lesson, and the critical thinking skills to determine the relative merits and faults of the lesson. Students sometimes need to be elevated to a higher level of interest and urgency. This is more than simply telling students they will be tested on the information. The best way to create interest and urgency is to create a learning environment that requires students to acquire and use their knowledge and skills in order to participate in it. For example, the teacher could prepare a lesson about fractions, but instead of simply drilling students with fraction worksheets, the teacher informs the class that they are going to operate a pizza parlor and sell pizza by the slice for lunch. They have to know how many slices per pizza, and how many total pizzas they will need. In this way, the teacher challenges students' thinking and creates what is known as "cognitive dissonance," or enough of an uncomfortable feeling that will motivate students to do something about it. They will figure it out and in the process learn what fractions are all about.

As a final comment on critical thinking, since teachers spend most of their time asking questions, care must be taken to devise questions that scaffold Costa's Levels of Inquiry (1 easy, 2 medium, and 3 hard) and then utilize these questions in such a way as to help all students, not just the ones listening. These types of questions should be prepared in advance. The easiest way to do this is to prepare a question card to carry with you as you do your direct instruction. Use the question card to prompt you to create questions that not only check for understanding (which is the first level of the scaffold), but also promote higher-order thinking (remember that thinking promotes memory).

Notes

1   George Lucas' adventure movie, *Indiana Jones and the Last Crusade,* had a character, Walter Donovan played by Julian Glover, who said those exact words to Dr. Jones, and he turned out to be the one who manipulated Dr. Jones and his father, Dr. Jones.
2   Students love to figure out puzzles, though they are almost identical to the dreaded "word problems" in math. Here is a process puzzle for you to puzzle through. A surgeon in a remote village only has two pairs of sterile rubber gloves left and he wants to get as many operations done before he has to stop. What can he do to get the most number of operations with only two pairs of sterile gloves? For more intriguing "lateral" puzzles (and the answer), check out Paul Sloane's books http://www.destination-innovation.com/the-top-ten-lateral-thinking-puzzles/
3   Our hippocampus is the organizing organ for saving and retrieving our memories especially emotional ones. It is in the center of the brain under corpus callosum (the part that allows the two halves to talk to each other, and also holds the two hemispheres together). This area of the brain is called the limbic system and is known to handle emotions, and memory. Visit the Psych Education site for an easy to read explanation: http://psycheducation.org/brain-tours/memory-learning-and-emotion-the-hippocampus/.
4   In J.K. Rowling's book, the *Half-Blood Prince*, the protagonist, Harry Potter, obtains a potions book full of marginal notes that help him master complicated mixtures and improve his usually poor performance in that class.
5   I learned about Cornell Notes when I became acquainted with AVID, a program to support and promote students going to college and being successful. I wondered why it was called Cornell Notes. They could only tell me that it came from Cornell University. I did some digging and found this out. In 1950, Dr. Walter Pauk, an education professor at Cornell University, wrote a book called *How to Study in College* (now in its 11th edition). It was adopted by Mary Catherine Swanson, founder of AVID, in the 1980s. It is still used and promoted at Cornell University (see http://lsc.cornell.edu/study-skills/cornell-note-taking-system/) and it is still a cornerstone of the AVID program. Watch this video: https://www.youtube.com/watch?v=73W7d8-Rl1E&feature=youtube).
6   Vanderbilt University's Center for Teaching has a marvelous web page on metacognition: https://cft.vanderbilt.edu/guides-sub-pages/metacognition/. It explains what it is and how to do it in detail. BTW metacognition is only one of almost 100 encyclopedic "teaching guides" available gratis.
7   An interesting discussion of the true cause of the seasons can be found at the Annenberg Foundation media website: www.learner.org/resources/series28.html (click on the VoD symbol to watch the movie). This is a video produced by the Harvard-Smithsonian Center for Astrophysics in 1987. There are also math and science activities and lessons that go along with this program, called Minds of Our Own and Private Universe.
8   Shel Silverstein wrote several books that can be found at http://www.shelsilverstein.com/books/. My favorite is *Where The Sidewalk Ends*. One of the poems and humorous illustrations is that of Melinda Mae who decides she will eat a whale and by the time she was 89 she finally finished it. Sometimes the morals of the poems are straightforward, while at other times they just make you laugh.

References

Albergaria Almeida, P. (2010). Questioning Patterns, Questioning Profiles and Teaching Strategies in Secondary Education. *International Journal of Learning, 17*(1), 587–600. doi:10.1504/IJLC.2010.035833.

The College Board Standards for College Success in Mathematics and Statistics: Adapted for Integrated Curricula. (2007). Retrieved March 25th, 2017 from http://www.collegeboard.com/prod_downloads/about/association/academic/Integrated_Math_Standards.pdf.

Costa, A. (2011). *Costa's Levels of Inquiry*. Retrieved March 20th, 2012 from *www.fresno.k12.ca.us/divdept/sscience/.../CostaQuestioning.pdf*.

Dossett, D. and Burns, B. (2000). The Development of Children's Knowledge of Attention and Resource Allocation in Single and Dual Tasks. *Journal of Genetic Psychology, 161*(2), 216–34. Retrieved September 5th, 2009, from Research Library. (Document ID: 54901844).

Fox, M. (2001). *Reading Magic: Why Reading Aloud to Our Children Will Change Their Lives Forever*. Orlando, FL: Harcourt.

Lucas, G. (Producer), Spielberg, S. (Director). (1989). *Indiana Jones and the Last Crusade* [Motion picture]. USA: Lucasfilm.

Marzano, R., Pickering, D., and Pollock, J. (2001). *Classroom Instruction That Works: Research-Based Strategies for Increasing Student Achievement.* Alexandria, VA: Association for Supervision and Curriculum Development.

Rowe, M. B. (1974). Wait-time and Rewards as Instructional Variables, Their Influence on Language, Logic, and Fate Control: Part One–Wait-time. *Journal of Research in Science Teaching, 11*, 81–94.

Rowe, M. B. (1987). Wait Time: Slowing Down May be a Way of Speeding Up. *American Educator, 11*, 38–48.

Rowling, J. K. (2005). *Harry Potter and the Half-Blood Prince.* New York, NY: Arthur A. Levine Books.

Schmoker, M. (2006). *Results Now: How We Can Achieve Unprecedented Improvements in Teaching and Learning*. Alexandria, VA: Association of Supervision and Curriculum Development.

Silverstein, S. (1974). *Where the Sidewalk Ends*. New York, NY: HarperCollins Publishers.

Tienken, C., Goldberg, S., and DiRocco, D. (2012). Questioning the Questions. *Kappa Delta Pi Record*. http://dx.doi.org/10.1080/00228958.2009.10516690.

Willingham, D. (2010). *Why Don't Students Like School: A Cognitive Scientist Answers Questions about How the Mind Works and What It Means for Schools*. San Francisco, CA: Jossey-Bass.

Zhang, M., Lundeberg, M., McConnell, T. J., Koehler, M. J., and Eberhardt, J. (2010). Using Questioning to Facilitate Discussion of Science Teaching Problems in Teacher Professional Development. *Interdisciplinary Journal of Problem-Based Learning, 4*(1), 57–82. doi:10.1007/s10972-009-9161-8.

Chapter 3

Problem Solvers

Utilizes Analytical and Critical Tools to Arrive at Solutions

Why Do Students Need to Be Problem Solvers?

I learned something about myself and about students when I was at a "Fathers and Sons" campout with my son, Gideon, and his friend, T.J. One of the fireside activities included an interlocking rope puzzle that Gideon and T.J. became very eager to solve. The puzzle was the one where a rope is tied around each of your wrists and your partner has a different rope tied around his wrists, but the puzzle is that your ropes are interconnected in the middle. The task is to get separated without untying the ropes from your wrists. The boys witnessed that it could be done, but they did not see how it was done. This piqued their curiosity as a video game could never have done, and they both became determined to figure it out, no matter how long it took.

So Gideon and his friend T.J., who were 15 years old at the time, worked at this puzzle for a good half hour. It was interesting to watch them contort and twist, trying to get the ropes disconnected. Perhaps even more interesting was my reaction to this situation. I knew the answer to the puzzle and part of me desired, more than anything, to share this knowledge. But each time I anxiously asked them if they wanted help, Gideon and T.J. were emphatic, "No help!" So I tried unsuccessfully to content myself with holding the flashlight as they tried one idea after another.

While I watched them, I learned a marvelous truth: The motivation to arrive at the solution to the puzzle was far greater than the motivation to receive a candy bar, the prize for solving the puzzle. Considering we are talking about ravenous teenage boys, that discovery is amazing. As Gideon and T.J. continued to work on the puzzle, they noticed that some other boys were doing the same puzzle but were much younger, and their motivation, I believe, was less pure. They wanted the candy bars, unlike Gideon and T.J., to whom the treats were secondary. Worst of all, these younger boys were solving the puzzle (I believe they got help). This only spurred my son and his friend on to more fevered twisting and tangling of ropes while it cankered me that I was not allowed to help. I was anxious to help because I knew the answer. With a few simple words, I could help them be successful.

Then I thought, "Why do I want so badly to share this knowledge? Is it to help them, or is it for me?" I was shocked at the realization that, in truth, my motivation was all about me. I wanted to show them how much I knew and how smart I was, more than I wanted them to succeed on their own.

With this realization, I had no trouble keeping my mouth shut, and I let the boys enjoy their learning adventure. A thought did occur to me, though. If I could not help them, perhaps I could get them thinking in the right direction. After all, it was getting late and who knew how much longer it would take them.

I simply asked a question. "How many circles of rope did you say there were?"

"Two!"

"Are you sure?"

"Yes! See! One, t- … wait a minute. There are … four … no … there are six! Oh, I get it!"

Their progress became much faster and they eventually figured it out. Most importantly, they did it without my help. For these young men, that made all the difference, and it made the victory chocolate that much sweeter.

After this experience, it got me thinking about my teaching. When I slave over a lesson plan and create great questions and conversation points, I sometimes put more value on *my* knowledge and experience that *I* want to impart, rather than on the significantly greater knowledge and experience that the *students* will gain if I let them make discoveries on their *own*. Then the little devil gets on my shoulder and says, "But that takes more planning and more preparation. It is so much easier just to tell them what they need to learn. After all, why reinvent the wheel?"

Pure discovery is the true "student-centered" strategy but few teachers have the luxury of allotting all of their time to letting students "roust around" discovering everything. Most often, because of time constraints, dedicated teachers create a few isolated discovery-learning situations as if they were bubbles in a sea of teacher-centered curriculum. But even then, many teachers feel the need to just give the students the answers—either when students reflexively ask for them, or when the teacher, in frustration, just proffers them when not asked. We forget that allowing students to reinvent the wheel creates better wheels ... and smarter students. I am reminded of the seagulls that forgot how to fish because of hanging around the fishermen. As much as we feel we are being philanthropic with our fish, we are, in fact, feeding our own egos and in essence creating a dependence that will ultimately lead towards intellectual starvation! When teachers constantly answer student questions, we are actually harming the students more than helping them.

The solution is straightforward and at the same time extremely difficult: When we are faced with the temptation to "help" students, we have to be strong enough to *close our mouths* at the right times! We have to quit saying, "Let me show you." We have to learn to say, "That is interesting. What do you think? Have you thought about this?" And we have to swallow our pride to lie and say, "I don't know. Find out for yourself. You might try looking here." (In reality, sometimes we do not know the solution, but that is a dangerous place to remain as an educator. We really should know the answers and we should model what we want the students to do—i.e., do the research.)

Not directing and controlling students will be made harder because some students, especially the older ones, will say, "Just tell me what I need to know to pass the test!" You see, our system has trained them to sit quietly and wait for the teacher to give the answers to the predetermined questions. Savvy teachers will have to do some "de-culturalization" and help these students learn how to "discover" on their own before these students will be able to benefit from this method. Establishing the habit of getting students to ask questions and search for answers takes 21 days, just as it does for any habit. The rewards of this simple change of thinking will endure much longer in the habits of mind we create in our students.

Gideon and T.J. had a blast at the "Fathers and Sons" outing. They experienced success in learning as they solved the rope puzzle, and because of that, they will be emboldened to tackle even harder challenges. I am glad that I kept my ego in check and did not rob them of that success by selfishly revealing the solution.

Often, mathematics is the main focus of problem solving. The ACT organized its standards according to the scores that require them. For example, in order to get a perfect score[1] on the writing section of the ACT test a student must be able to develop a topic that includes a complex purpose that meets the identified goal of the essay, and uses words and phrases that accomplish complex purpose (see Figure 3.1). None of that will happen without analytical, critical, and creative thinking, A.K.A. problem solving.

All of the boldface behaviors in the excerpt in Figure 3.1 relate to problem-solving skills. Note that analytical thinking is required for arriving at

Figure 3.1 *ACT Writing Standards (Excerpt from ACT College and Career Readiness Standards)* (Emphasis Added)

	Score Range	Score Range	Score Range	Score Range	Score Range	Score Range
	13–15	16–19	20–23	24–27	28–32	33–36
Topic Development in Terms of Purpose and Focus (TOD)	TOD 201. Delete material because it is obviously irrelevant in terms of the topic of the essay	TOD 301. **Delete material because it is obviously irrelevant in terms of the focus of the essay**	TOD 401. **Determine relevance** of material in terms of the focus of the essay	TOD 501. **Determine relevance** of material in terms of the focus of the paragraph	TOD 601. **Determine relevance** when considering material that is plausible but potentially irrelevant at a given point in the essay	TOD 701. **Identify the purpose** of a word, phrase, or sentence when the purpose is complex (e.g., anticipating a reader's need for background information) or requires a thorough understanding of the paragraph and essay
		TOD 302. Identify the purpose of a word or phrase when the purpose is simple (e.g., identifying a person, defining a basic term, using common descriptive adjectives)	TOD 402. **Identify the purpose** of a word or phrase when the purpose is straightforward (e.g., describing a person, giving examples)	TOD 502. **Identify the purpose** of a word, phrase, or sentence when purpose is fairly straightforward (e.g., identifying traits, giving reasons, explaining motivations)	TOD 602. **Identify the purpose** of a word, phrase, or sentence when the purpose is subtle (e.g., supporting a later point, establishing tone) or when the best decision is to delete the text in question	TOD 702. **Determine whether a complex essay has met a specified goal**
		TOD 303. Determine whether a simple essay has met a straightforward goal	TOD 403. Use a word, phrase, or sentence to accomplish a straightforward purpose (e.g., conveying a feeling or attitude)	TOD 503. **Determine whether an essay has met a specified goal**	TOD 603. **Use a word, phrase, or sentence to accomplish a subtle purpose** (e.g., adding emphasis or supporting detail, expressing meaning through connotation)	TOD 703. **Use a word, phrase, or sentence to accomplish a complex purpose,** often in terms of the focus of the essay
				TOD 504. Use a word, phrase, or sentence to accomplish a fairly straightforward purpose (e.g., sharpening an essay's focus, illustrating a given statement)		

"Delete" and critical thinking to be able to "Determine" are both required to effectively problem solve. Also notice that the higher the scores, the more problem solving and creative thinking is occurring.

Thinking Tools

As you recall, the cognitive scientist, Daniel Willingham, points out that although human beings are not very good at "thinking," we love to do it. What we are really good at, however, is making sense of things, even if what we figure out is incorrect (remember Aristotle?). We have a deep need to have explanations for things, even if they are way off base. In the movie *Private Universe* from the Annenburg Foundation, a girl in the video had some crazy explanation on how the seasons came about, and it made sense to her. It was wrong, but it explained things in her way of thinking so she felt satisfied. Earlier we learned that cognitive dissonance has to occur in order for this wrong thinking to change; otherwise we stick with our first theory. So the first step of effective problem solving is making correct sense of what is going on that is causing the problem. The Design Thinking teams at Stanford University would call that "empathy."[2] Gaining that understanding requires analytical thinking. The second part of problem solving is determining the causes of the problem. The final part is finding solutions. This requires critical thinking (evaluative) and creative (synthesizing) thinking skills. Effective problem solvers use the three thinking tools as a master mechanic uses socket wrenches, screw drivers, and alignment tools. As my father would always tell me, "Use the right tool for the job and the job is easier." Because analytical thinking, critical thinking, and problem solving are not interchangeable tools, knowing their functions will help students match the right thinking tool to the task at hand.

Creativity Is the Key to Effective Problem Solving

Since analytical and critical thinking (essential elements of problem solving) have already been discussed in the how section of this chapter, we will discuss what it takes to arrive at a solution: creativity. Given that we already understand the parts and pieces of a situation and that we have already determined the source of the problem, the only thing left is finding a solution or resolution to the problem. Problem-solving heuristics abound, but all of them have similar formats: Investigate, Define the Problem, Research Solutions, Identify the Best Solution, and Implement the Solution. In this case, we are focusing on the last few actions of the problem-solving algorithms: identifying options and choosing the best solution. Now that doesn't mean that analysis and criticism are not going to be used anymore, it just means that they are in the background. What brain power is necessary to identify options and possible solutions? *Creativity*.

Yikes! When the word "creativity" is used, the left side of my head begins to hurt. Why would that happen? Hmm … let me see, could it be the years of exposure to right- and left-brain mumbo jumbo? In this book, we are not interested in developing one side or the other of your brain; we want to develop all of the brain. This is possible because the brain is a seamlessly integrated whole, and as neuroscientists have discovered, no part of the brain works in isolation. If you want to see some interesting things about the brain, there is an iTunes University course on the brain from the University of Arizona, called Visualizing Human Thought, that shows that even though a man had nearly his entire left hemisphere destroyed by a stroke, including the comprehension (Wernike's area) and speech center (Broca's area), he can still communicate. How? According to right-left brain theories, he shouldn't be able to. Well, what happened was that his brain adapted and found a way to use another part of the brain to take over the job (it is an enthralling story). The point is that thinking—in this case problem solving—is a "whole-brain" activity.

Literacy and CCR

The fruit of education is literacy and this in itself suggests a way to get to the heart of problem solving. When you say that someone is literate, you are not just saying they know how to read. You are saying much more than that. Being literate means being well read or having read a lot. Not only that, but there is an assumption that literate individuals have acquired knowledge gained from reading. This knowledge has become part of them and is used both to support and to contradict what this literate person believes or doesn't believe. A literate person, therefore, has ready evidence upon which to base beliefs and sufficient ammunition to argue against other beliefs. In similar fashion, problem solvers must be literate about the problem and the solutions. This is the first step in problem solving.

A person charged with solving a problem must have investigated the problem from various angles and sources in order to comprehend the problem and along the way have gathered sufficient evidence to bolster conclusions one way or another about the problem. The Stanford Design Thinking process starts with Empathy, or in other words, knowing your problem so well that you can empathize with those people suffering from it. Following this train of thought, we could call this first stage of problem solving "problem literacy." Thus, being literate about the problem, the individual is ready to creatively find solutions. In chapter 10 we will discuss literacy in more depth but for now it is important that we understand that in terms of problem solving, any person can read a narrative and an explanatory piece of literature and accept at face value the information obtained because only one side is presented. But an argument requires a totally different reading skill because the literate person will not concede any points without substantial evidence (and as you will see later in this chapter and in chapter 10, the ability to read arguments effectively is a precursor to writing arguments effectively). You might think that colleges and universities establish argument as foundational to any study. Both argument and reasoning are tools for persuasion used in advertising and sales room. An effective argument requires logical evidence to convince another person and may utilize more subtle means, such as authority, expert witnesses, emotions, or the sympathies of the reader as is found in advertising.

I must point out that neither argument nor reasoning is necessarily based on truth. They are used to promote an individual's point of view and personal biases (Mercier, 2011).

Reading Is the Basis of Learning Problem Solving

An excellent author is capable of presenting readers with arguments because of the amassed knowledge and thinking skills acquired as part of becoming literate. The reader must have similar skills to unravel the arguments and the evidence. That is the true enjoyment of reading: being able to see the author's point of view and then to determine if you agree with it or not. In the ACT's report, Reading Between the Lines, only half of students who took the reading test passed at what the ACT would call the acceptable level. A score of 21 or better means that 85 percent of those students have a good chance of getting at least a "C" in history or psychology at a university or college (ACT, 2006, p. 11).

I am going to say something earthshattering that no one has ever said before: effective reading is critical for our students to be ready for college and the workforce of today and the future. OK, you got me. This has been the basis of hundreds of books and reports (ACT, 2006, p. 27), but it is so fundamental it is often overlooked. It is through reading complex literature that students can discover the power of argument and problem solving.

How does reading an argument help students solve problems? A problem solved must be compelling enough to need a solution. The solution to a problem must be believable, plausible, and doable. An effective solution to a problem is irrefutable because it works! Texts worthy of being read show problems that are solved in intriguing and convoluted ways. These types of text establish a reason to read them and draw the reader into the situation (I use the word "text" loosely to mean literature as well as explanatory or informational text, narratives, and arguments that have a more academic purpose). Students who learn how to read these types of texts learn how to solve problems from multitudes of perspectives. This literature is complex and to be ready for college and careers, students need to be well practiced.

According to research done by ACT (2006), while the complexity of college reading is rising, the complexity of K–12 reading is diminishing. ACT compares the reading comprehension scores of high school students who did not read complex literature. "The most important implication of this study was that a pedagogy focused only on 'higher-order' or 'critical' thinking was insufficient to ensure that students were ready for college and careers: what students could read, in terms of its complexity, was at least as important as what they could do with what they read." So it makes sense that as we prepare students with a "higher-order thinking" curriculum, we must make sure they are given opportunities to read more complex literature. Complex literature is defined by the RSVP method (ACT, p. 15), as shown in Figure 3.2.

The 2006 ACT study found some other interesting facts by looking at the relationship between the complexity of the reading and the test scores on the ACT (see Figure 3.3). Researchers discovered that the more questions a student answers correctly on the ACT Reading test, the higher their ACT Reading score (a scale of 1–36). Duh, right? What was interesting, though, was what they found when they took those same scores and related them to the complexity of the text. As it turns out, all students with an ACT score under 21 were able to answer correctly about 30 percent of the questions from a complex text, regardless of their ACT Reading scores. What this means is that students will understand complex texts at the same level, regardless of their other reading skills. Above an ACT Reading score of 21, an exponential relationship develops: as the ACT Reading score increases, the percentage of correctly answered questions concerning complex texts gradually increases. This signifies that there is a threshold that limits student success on reading-skills tests, and that obtaining skills in reading complex texts is the deciding factor.

To put it more simply, either students can effectively interpret complex texts or they can't. Once they learn how to effectively read complex texts,

Figure 3.2 ACT's RSVP Method for Classifying Complex Literature

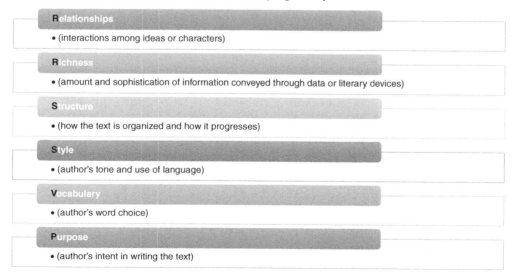

Relationships
- (interactions among ideas or characters)

Richness
- (amount and sophistication of information conveyed through data or literary devices)

Structure
- (how the text is organized and how it progresses)

Style
- (author's tone and use of language)

Vocabulary
- (author's word choice)

Purpose
- (author's intent in writing the text)

Figure 3.3 Relation of Exposure to Complex Literature to Performance on ACT Test

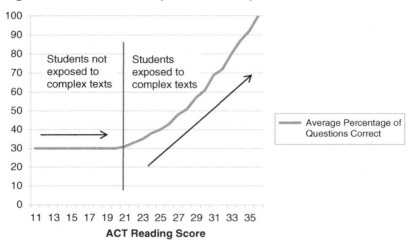

only intensive practice will make a difference in their ACT Reading scores. As shown in Figure 3.3, it appears that a score of 21 and above on the ACT Reading test is a reliable predictor of college-readiness and that adequately preparing students to read complex texts can dramatically increase their ACT Reading scores (ACT, 2006, p. 15).

In order to prepare students for college, educators need to get students reading arguments rather than simple narrative, they need to read opposing sides of history instead of the myopic textbooks, they need to engage in scientific debates that fueled discovery and mathematical disagreements that inspired chaos. The argument students read must be compelling, believable, and relevant in every subject—and these arguments are out there; we just have to find them. I am not saying that we have to create controversy. I am saying that in order to understand and then make a decision, students need the full or at least both sides of the story.

Now it is time to put all of this all together. Becoming literate is related to being an effective problem solver, which will help your students be college- and career-ready. In order to solve a problem, students must be literate in the problem—they must have the necessary background information upon which to build an argument of understanding.[3] Then with this knowledge, students can seek solutions. I use the word "solution" deliberately because it relates to effective arguments. This reminds me of a fifth-grade science class at George Gervin Academy in San Antonio. They learned a definition of "solution" through a student-created and -choreographed chant: "A solution is a mixture of two or more compounds that cannot be easily separated." If we apply that definition, the solution to a problem should be so integrated, like the brain (see, I did not forget where this started), so that the parts and pieces are not easily separated. The solution is unified or integrated, just like an effective argument should be.

Literary Problem Solving Using RSVP

Oh, you want an example? Here it goes. One of my favorite books, *The Count of Monte Cristo* by Alexandre Dumas, has all of the RSVP elements of complexity. As far as problem solving, there are several intriguing problems to be solved in the storyline, but Edmond's problem is the biggest. You know the story: just as Edmond was going to have a "happy ever after," everything was stolen from him. The problem: Edmond seeks resolution of his fiendish capture and imprisonment. Then later seeks retribution and revenge? OK, he could have them eliminated. That would be the easy solution. The real problem with which Edmond wrestled was how to destroy people's lives and make them suffer as he had suffered. Edmond's ultimate retribution was that his enemies would know that he was responsible for their suffering. Edmond first had to identify motives for his supposed friends' behavior, and then identify their methods. Why did they move against Edmond in the first place? The answer to that would be fear, envy, greed, and power: fear of being discovered with ties to Bonaparte, envy that Edmond was going to be "captain" and married (in other words—happy), and greed for being able to take Edmond's place and the accompanying monetary possibilities. The final motivation was the mutually beneficial interest in disposing of Edmond to retain power by eliminating loose ends. While Edmond is in prison, he figures this out. In the end, he believes that payback, in all fairness, should be on the same terms. This means that he must take away their happiness, their money, and their power, and in doing all this, make them very afraid. Of course, it is easy to look at problem solving in this way, because I know how the story ends. With unknown endings it is much more challenging.

In the strategies and techniques that follow, I will use literature to help you teach your students effective problem-solving strategies and techniques. (You were probably expecting mathematics or science problems to solve; sorry to disappoint you.) You may agree, or disagree, but reading about Edmond's argument is compelling. It is made doable with the incredible fortune he inherited, and as the story unfolds, it is irrefutable—Edmond does what he set out to do. Of course, there are other interesting things to discuss about this story: Is the terrifying transformation of Edmond worth the cost? Does Edmond not become what he is trying to destroy? You get the drift.

How to Help Students Become Successful Problem Solvers

S T R A T E G Y

Methods for Inciting Creativity and Identifying Options for Solving Problems

Wouldn't it be nice if we had a creativity pill full of playfulness, irreverence, rule-bending, and flubber[4] every time we needed creativity to solve a problem? The thing about creativity is that it is not like recalling a fact or remembering a situation. Though like memory, it requires intense mental effort that is directed at a problem; unlike memory, there is no guarantee the effort will produce results. With problem solving, sometimes we have creativity forced upon us. Dire circumstances and desperation can make us creative. Other times, responding to less critical motivators such as peer pressure, laziness, ambition, and shame can inspire creativity. But most of all, being creative means coming up with a variety of options from which we can choose to go about solving problems, for whatever reason. But these options are not pulled out of thin air. Our personal experiences, memories, knowledge of the situation, and knowledge of similar situations all affect our ability to engage creativity to devise options for solving a problem. The more options that are created, the more opportunities we will have for successful resolution of the problem. The following techniques are shared to identify problem-solving options but can also be used for other creative learning opportunities with a little adjustment. Most of the techniques for teaching this strategy are take-offs on what we call brainstorming for solutions.

TECHNIQUE: Word association. This is a variation of a couple of popular word games called Boggle and Password. The point of the game is to come up with as many unique words related to the word in question as possible. A sixth-grade teacher would flash a word on the screen from a great book, let's say *Belle Prater's Boy* by Ruth White, that has just been read.

The topic is "Why does Woodrow tell stories?" The students in teams of two to four have to come up with as many related words or phrases from the book as possible. Examples: "They're funny," "They're scary," "They're short." After students run out of easy words, they have to think harder: "true," "make-believe," "he likes fairytales," "he's sad," "to make fun of," "he lies," "to make Gypsy happy," "mother's ghost," "he's afraid," "for protection," "he's like his mother." Students have only one minute. After the time is up, the teams one-by-one share the words they have written down. As a word or phrase is read, if another group has it, then everyone has to scratch it out. If no one has the word or phrase, and the class agrees that it is related to the topic, everyone circles it. After the last team has read their words, then the team with the most unique words wins.

TECHNIQUE: Inkblot (Rorschach) test. This is more of an arts and crafts type of creativity technique. Students make spots of ink (several colors work best) on paper and fold the paper in half, squishing it completely flat. Then they open the paper and write a paragraph or two on what they see from various angles. To make this more interesting, the teacher chooses a book or story, like Edgar Allan Poe's "Cask of Amontillado," and students have to come up with at least four different icons of the story related to their inkblot. For each icon, students should describe how it connects to the story. Examples: "motivation," "humiliation," "enticement of the cask," "fear of the catacombs," "humor the jester," "revenge of Montressor." Another twist would be to take the perspective of one of the characters and try to determine how he or she would interpret the inkblot, or take the perspective of the author and how he or she would interpret the inkblot.

TECHNIQUE: Astronomer's view. This technique is taking the birds' eye view to its logical limit The point is to look for patterns (constellations) in the surrounding stars. Many times solutions appear as we step back from the problem (way back) and identify the big picture and what is around it. To do this, we need to ask questions like, "Why was the book written?" "What did the author want from readers?" "Who did the author think would read this book?" "What other books are like this one?" "How did the author's life affect his writing?" In *Journey to the Center of the Earth* by Jules Verne, some of the big pictures are these: "Back in Mr. Verne's time, did they believe that it was possible to have a world at the center of the earth?" "What did they know about dinosaurs back then compared to what we know now?" "What other books did Jules Verne write?" "Why are all of Jules Verne's books adventures?" "Was Jules Verne describing his own time period accurately, or was that the future for him?" "What did Verne think about the future?" "What options did Jules Verne have to solve the problems he presented in his book?" "How have those options changed?" "If you were a Vernian (i.e., someone who believed that Jules Verne actually experienced his adventures), what would you want to find most?" Depending on the age of your students, you could either ask the questions yourself and put them on a WebQuest page for students to investigate, or teach the technique and have students ask the astronomer questions and then answer their own questions.

TECHNIQUE: *Atomic view*. The atomic view looks at a story through the eyes of an electron microscope into the very structure of the words spinning madly around the ideas. Students look at word choice, style, spelling, rhythms, meter and fluency in order to elucidate possible meanings and motives of the author. For example, *A Connecticut Yankee in King Arthur's Court* by Mark Twain deals with two colliding time periods. Sophomore English classes could list the words used by the "Boss" and then list the vocabulary of the knights and make some stunning conclusions. By asking, posing, or providing questions like the following, even more discussion about word choice and intended interpretation would ensue: "How did the Boss overcome the difficulty of describing something with which he was very familiar, but the knights knew nothing about because it hadn't been invented yet?" "What part did the culture play in not only the choice of words used, but also how those words were placed in sentences (rhythms, meter, phraseology)?" "Some of the words used by the knights were Old English and are not used in modern language; how did Twain write so readers would understand them?" "How did Twain illustrate the thinking, ideology, and culture of the people in the time of Camelot?" "What level of language did Twain use to narrate the story?" Students could create a spreadsheet of the different language characteristics of each type of individual in the story in order to compare and categorize the words used. They could demonstrate how Twain effectively or ineffectively represented different castes and education levels among the people of Camelot.

TECHNIQUE: *Bubble test*. Just as the name suggests, this technique gathers what floats to the top first and then categorizes the ideas as they come along. Through a group histogram (frequency analysis), we can determine which bubbles are larger in terms of priority or popularity than others by how many groups come up with the same idea. This can be done as a group activity or individually, but it is more fun in a group. If the book that is being read in a fifth-grade class is *Baseball in April and Other Stories* by Gary Soto, then each group can take a chapter and identify the problems encountered by Alfonzo, Hector, Michael, and Veronica. Students could then identify the solutions in groups, then add their conclusions to the whiteboard histogram.

TECHNIQUE: Gallery walk. Each group of four or five students creates a poster representing the best symbolism of the literature. For example, eighth graders would be able to identify the problems (plots) and the effectiveness of the solutions in the book *The War of the Worlds* by H. G. Wells. For example: "Confronted with the reality that man is insignificant compared to more advanced beings," "Fear of being caught and the motivation of survival," "Human desire to fight back against impossible odds," "Witness the metamorphosis of humanity when placed in dire circumstances," "Revelation of what is most important in this life," "Struggling with despair." Once the posters are displayed on the walls, each group stands up and travels about the room, critiquing each poster. On sticky notes, each group writes a question or makes a comment. After all the posters have been reviewed, each group looks at the comments and writes a reflection about what they learned by reviewing other posters, and what they learned by reading the comments and questions of the other groups.

STRATEGY

Design Thinking

First of all, what is Design Thinking? Design Thinking is a structured group process that incorporates failure into the process and frequently causes the designers to go back to the beginning and start from scratch. Design Thinking begins as a design process in which multiple options are considered all at once and then tested. Failure is anticipated and incorporated as a key element to improving the designs or plans. Design Thinking is successful when the designer finally creates a working prototype and failures along the way bring the process closer and closer to that goal.[5] There are several Design Thinking models, here are three of the most commonly found in educational contexts. Common to each model is the idea of improving the design over multiple iterations.

TECHNIQUE: Express, Test, Cycle (McKim, 1973).[6] Any Design Thinking process follows a cyclical pattern that expects several iterations in order to perfect the design. Express, Test, and Cycle design steps are excellent for novice designers, especially young ones because there are only three easy-to-understand steps. Groups of three or four novice design students can easily remember the three steps as they work through the process. It is also easy for teachers to use these three steps to create design sheets that help the students record their ideas, their results, and what they learned for the next iteration.

In a math class, students may express a problem, "Learning to solve for the lowest common denominator is hard. Is there an easier way to learn how to do it?" Yes. Students need to follow a systematic approach to factoring the denominator. Student designers will create their process and a survey instrument to gather feedback. They will check to make sure the students answered the math correctly. If the student gets the answer right, then according to the designers, 80 percent "this helps me" responses on the survey would indicate success. The designers discuss the results of survey question and use the insight gained to either revise the original process or cycle and use one of the other design processes they had earlier discussed.[7]

TECHNIQUE: Plan, Do, Study, Act. Edward Deming was a master of creating efficient, thoughtful processes that helped businesses around the world improve. As part of its training of business managers, the Deming Institute uses the Plan, Do, Study, Act four-step process (PDSA Cycle).[8] This is also a good model for novice Design Thinkers, but it also has enough rigor to be able to support authentic research as a foundation for the design. Middle to high school students can use this model effectively. I like this model because the idea of a pilot test group, or prototype, is introduced.

Students in an English class may use the PDSA Cycle to help other students write persuasive essays. They do some research to identify what is the most persuasive essay and they create a template to help students write. They test it out and study the results. They repeat the process as necessary until they can say the tool helps students write better persuasive essays.

TECHNIQUE: Empathy, Define, Ideate, Prototype, Test. The Design Thinking model from the Institute of Design at Stanford is the *Empathy, Define, Ideate, Prototype, Test* process. The Stanford website includes sample design projects for elementary, middle, and high school.[9] This Design Thinking model can be for more advanced Design Thinkers because it requires designers to intensely prepare for the actual design. After this preparation the steps of Ideate, Prototype, and Test become a sub-cycle to the entire process. Like all Design Thinking models, iteration and testing are the keys to arriving at the best designs.

After observing (empathizing in) science classes, students may notice that "Some boys typically struggle in acquiring scientific terminology." They would then define the problem as "Teen age boys need to acquire the scientific vocabulary to be able to discuss discovered knowledge, propose correct hypotheses, and carry out successful experiments." In Ideating (or generating ideas) two ideas percolate to the top: "Boys would rather be outside playing sports. Boys are not concerned with precision, close enough is fine." These are made into simple prototype telephone apps and tested.

S T R A T E G Y

Lateral Thinking

In the world of geometry, oblique angles are those that are either more or less than 90 degrees. However, when using "oblique" in other ways, it means something that comes at you diagonally, not straight on. The purpose of this strategy is not to deal with the issue in front of us, but the side issues that might surprise us if we took note of them. This is called lateral thinking[10] (not to be confused with lateral learning, or learning from your peers or clients, also known as co-creation).

Thinking "out of the box" is such a worn-out phrase, but the concept remains vital, though the way to do that has eluded us, kind of like picking ourselves up by the bootstraps. Lateral thinking involves a process and a series of thinking tools that contradict the prevalent attitude that creativity just happens serendipitously, out of the blue, and the solution falls into your lap. Creativity is hard work, hard mental work.

TECHNIQUE: Flashlight. Wherever the light shines (use a light that can focus the beam), that is the point of interest. T. H. White's "The Sword in the Stone" in *The Once and Future King* is the perfect opportunity to use this technique. The teacher will have to make sign cards of the characters or topics to be used. Let's shine the light on Merlyn. The teacher has prepared questions for discussion such as, "Merlyn's problem was how to make

Wart into the king that Merlyn knew he would be. Similar to the game of *Jeopardy*, Merlyn had the answers, but he did not have the questions because he hadn't asked them yet."[11] While the light is shining on Merlyn, students identify the problems he had in training Wart, his difficulties with Sir Ector, etc. Then the teacher (or student) shines the light on Kay. Students now identify what problems Kay had to overcome to become a knight, how he dealt with the strange Wart, and how he overcame his shock when Wart was able to pull the sword out of the stone and he could not. The light could land on King Pellinore, or Archimedes, or the pike.

TECHNIQUE: SWOT. Using a process to identify patterns such as SWOT, which identifies strengths, weaknesses, opportunities, and threats, can help students lay the foundation for making decisions (evaluation in Bloom's Taxonomy) regarding possible courses of action and solutions. (see Figure 3.4) This technique is an expansion of the effective pro and con process used to organize thinking for persuasive (hortatory) writing. Not only do you utilize the pros (strengths) and cons (weaknesses), but the results of the choices are considered separately in opportunities and threats. An interesting analysis technique is to juxtapose these opposites in a table and force the analysis of the situation's possibilities concurrently. Lively discussion can ensue to determine which of the items belong to both strengths and opportunities, opportunities and weaknesses, threats and strengths, and threats and weaknesses.

TECHNIQUE: KWL (What do I know? What do I want to know? What did I learn?) KWL and its many variations were designed and are most powerful as pre-reading strategies to help students prepare for reading by anticipating information that might be in the reading selection. Students do this by looking at clues such as pictures on the book's cover, the book's title and author, the table of contents, the back of the book, the introductory paragraph, etc. (Szabo, 2006). Then students must ask themselves," What

Figure 3.4   Strength/Weakness, Opportunity/Threat (SWOT) Decision Table

	Strength	Weakness
Opportunity		
Threat		

do I know (about what I am going to read)?" This first question has misled many teachers to use KWL as a pretesting method for different subjects because this first question is the basis of any pretest—to find out what students know before teaching begins. However, I must clarify that this question is focused solely on the information gathered from looking at the cover of the book, flipping a few pages, interpreting the title, and knowing something about the author. The student will do some deductive thinking, again based on the perusal of the outside of the book, to guess what the book is about. Based on what they have just gleaned from the cover of the book or skimming the article, the students then ask themselves

"What do I want to know? "Or in other words, what has piqued my interest, or what am I curious to find out, or how has the author of this text invited me to know more? Students should answer this question not merely as matter of preference, but as a form of inquiry—"Why did the author write this book?" and "What am I to learn from it?" Some teachers are tempted to misuse this step and make the false assumption that students want to know about radioactive isotopes, the vertices of a triangle, or date of the battle of 1812.

Finally, after reading the selection, students write what was learned from the reading. KWL has been applied with various degrees of success as a pretesting procedure in many subjects, but as I've explained, it is most effective as a pre-reading strategy.

Notes

1　According to the ACT Profile Report—National of the Graduating Class of 2016, out of the over two million students who took the test, only 9,339 scored a perfect 36 on the English Language Arts tests (that's less than half of one percent!). The average score for the 519,922 students who took the optional writing portion was 19.3 out of 36. The data indicates that students are less proficient at writing than reading (22.9 average) and English (21.8 average).

2　Design Thinking at Stanford University follows a five-step design thinking process. One of the elements is empathy—or knowing your problem so well that you can empathize with those that suffer from it. Check out their website at https://dschool.stanford.edu/resources/chart-a-new-course-put-design-thinking-to-work.

3　An intriguing book supporting acquiring experience and background knowledge necessary for comprehension through first-hand field trips, and vicarious field trips, or in other words, reading, can be found in Marzano, R. J. (2004). *Building Background Knowledge for AcademicAchievement: Research on What Works in Schools*. Alexandria, Virginia: Association for Supervision and Curriculum Development.

4　Remember that series of Walt Disney movies about the "Absent-Minded Professor" (1961), played by Fred MacMurray? He accidentally invents "flubber" and finds a lot of interesting things that can be done with it. He puts it on the basketball team shoes, he puts it on the football, and he even puts it in his car to make it fly. Robin Williams starred in a remake of it (1997), but it was not nearly as good as the original.

5 If you are looking for a Design Thinking process that is proven to work in schools and provides training for the teachers and students, The Tools at Schools program is ideal. Dr. Don Buckley and his team work closely with the schools to create a program for the students. It has the added motivational factor of actually creating a finished, professionally constructed product. The hands-on elements incorporated from the beginning grab student interest and maintain it over a long period (25 weeks). Unfortunately, not every student project will be created. They use a modified Imagine, Design, Create process broken down into seven phases. The ultimate goal is to take the best designs from the students and send them to a manufacturer to be built or to a programmer to be created. The seven phases are: Introduction to the Project, Research and the Big Ideas, Final Design and Mock-Up, 3-D, Modeling, and Final Project Launch. Students have designed new highlighters, school folders, school furniture, lockers, and eating utensils. It doesn't have to be something tangible, it could also be virtual, as in a program, website, or app. Check out http://aruliden.com/work/aruliden-staples-back-to-school-2015-1 and also http://www.tools-at-schools.com/home.
6 See http://thinkingofdesign.blogspot.com/2014/08/kissing-design-thinking-process.html.
7 If you are looking for additional models, Dubberly (2005) wrote an e-book compendium of the many Design Thinking strategies that are vying for dominance. I personally like the simple model he mentions used by the Deming Institute: Plan, Do, Study, Act.
8 See: https://deming.org/management-system/pdsacycle.
9 For detailed explanations of the steps look at: https://www.interaction-design.org/literature/article/5-stages-in-the-design-thinking-process also for more information about the Hasso Platner Institute of Design at Stanford; see: http://dschool.stanford.edu/dgift/.
10 Lateral Thinking, first introduced by Dr. Edward De Bono in 1970, has produced a flurry of innovations in business and industry. Dr. Bono stated that improving does not mean dig the hole deeper. Another area you might investigate is that of Lateral Puzzles that present a simple scenario and only provide the minimum information for a lateral thinking solution. For a good introduction see http://www.destination-innovation.com/the-top-ten-lateral-thinking-puzzles/.
11 If you recall, Merlyn was the first Benjamin Button and lived his life backwards (actually, T.H. White published his book in 1958, while F. Scott Fitzgerald published his in 1922, so it is the other way around, but you understand what I mean). "The Curious Case of Benjamin Button" is an intriguing story from F. Scott Fitzgerald's book, *Tales of the Jazz Age*. In 2007, the story was made into a movie (www.imdb.com/title/tt0421715/) in which Brad Pitt played the tragic Benjamin Button. You can read the short story at www.readbookonline.net/read/690/10628/.

References

ACT (2016). Profile Report—National: Graduating Class of 2016. Retrieved March 25th, 2017 from https://www.act.org/content/dam/act/unsecured/documents/P_99_999999_N_S_N00_ACT-GCPR_National.pdf.

ACT (2006). Reading between the Lines: What the ACT Reveals about College Readiness in Reading. Retrieved March 25th, 2017 from http://www.act.org/content/dam/act/unsecured/documents/reading_report.pdf.

ACT College and Career Readiness Standards—English. Retrieved March 25th, 2017 from http://www.act.org/content/act/en/education-andcareer-planning/college-and-career-readiness-standards.html.

Chaffin, C. (Producer), Fincher, D. (Director). (2008). *The Curious Case of Benjamin Button* [Motion Picture]. USA: Warner Brothers.

Dahl, R. (1983). *The Witches.* New York, NY: Scholastic, Inc.

Disney, W. (Producer), Stephenson, R. (Director). (1961). *The Absent-Minded Professor* [Motion picture]. USA: Walt Disney Productions.

Dumas, A. (1845). *The Count of Monte Cristo*. Retrieved March 24th, 2017 from http://literature.org/authors/dumas-alexandre/the-count-of-monte-cristo/.

Fitzgerald, F. S. (1922). "The Curious Case of Benjamin Button" in *Tales of the Jazz Age* Retrieved May 25th, 2012 from http://www.pagebypagebooks.com/F_Scott_Fitzgerald/The_Curious_Case_Of_Benjamin_Button/.

Mercier, H. and Sperber, D. (2011). Why Do Humans Reason? Arguments for an Argumentative Theory. *Behavioral and Brain Sciences*, 34(2), 57–74; discussion 74–111. doi:http://dx.doi.org/10.1017/S0140525X10000968.

Twain, M. (1896). *A Connecticut Yankee in King Arthur's Court*. New York, NY: Aerie Books.

Verne, J. (1864). *Journey to the Center of the Earth*. New York, NY: Aerie Books.

Wells, H. G. (1938). *The War of the Worlds*. New York, NY: Aerie Books.

White, R. (1996). *Belle Prater's Boy*. New York, New York: Bantam Double Day Dell Books for Young Readers.

White, T. H. (1939). *The Once and Future King*. New York, NY: Ace Books.

Willingham, D. (2010). *Why Don't Students Like School: A Cognitive Scientist Answers Questions about How the Mind Works and What It Means for Schools*. San Francisco, CA: Jossey-Bass.

SECTION I
CONCLUSION

Thinking Can Be an Unbelievably Satisfying Learning Experience

I used to ask my daughter, Mercedes, when she was in junior high, "How was school?" I had learned to not ask yes or no questions, but she still habitually gave me a one-word answer: "Good." My typical reply was, "Good for what?" This made her laugh, but she still doesn't want to provide much detail about the day's learning activities. It might have been that she was providing a buffer of protection for her teachers from an overly critical dad, or I suppose it could have been a junior-high-age syndrome—simply not wanting dad to know too much. Whatever it was, "Good" was her typical response, and she only shared more after my insistent prodding. I thought at the time it would be nice if I asked, "How was school?" and she responded, "Unbelievably satisfying!"

Those are words that I don't think are regularly used to describe schools. Even more specifically, I am reasonably certain that in the history of the world, no student has ever described her day at school as "unbelievably satisfying." These are the thoughts that pass through my head every day as I drive past a billboard for Dr. Pepper, in which a smiling leprechaun holds up a soda can and in big, bold letters states, "Unbelievably Satisfying!" But wouldn't it be awesome if schools were able to inspire this kind of emotion in students?

So how could a regular, every day school experience be unbelievably satisfying to a student? Dr. Pepper claims it is unbelievably satisfying because it quenches your thirst, it is sweet, it is tasty, and it is fizzy. Let's look at how a teacher can make his or her learning activities unbelievably satisfying for students. Students have a general curiosity, a thirst to find out what's new. When a teacher inspires students to discover something new, you can actually hear the "gulp, gulp, gulp—ahhhhhhh." Students love to feel needed and essential. When teachers share leadership and play to the strengths of the student, there it goes again, "gulp, gulp, gulp—ahhhhhhh." Students crave honest and specific praise, and when they get it from an observant teacher, "gulp,

gulp, gulp—ahhhhhhh." The sweetness of victory fills students to the brim when they succeed at difficult problems with which an astute teacher has challenged them, "gulp, gulp, gulp—ahhhhhhh." Canny teachers purposefully engage students in hands-on projects designed to leave students with a taste for more, while energetic and enthusiastic teachers create fun and active learning environments where students' excitement can't help but bubble to the surface, "gulp, gulp, gulp—ahhhhhhh." That is how teachers can create unbelievably satisfying days at school for students.

Students need to feel like they are part of something extraordinary. School is hard work, but it doesn't have to be ordinary. In this chapter, we have explored ways in which learning using analytical thinking, critical thinking, and problem solving can make the learning experience extraordinary and "unbelievably satisfying." We discussed how teachers must focus on these three important thinking skills to develop literacy and mathematics skills in a way that encourages deeper learning rather than wider learning (that's only an inch deep).

Finally, getting away from the idea that education is something you do to students, and embracing the idea that it is something to be experienced with students, is what will make the difference between a "good" day at school and an "unbelievably satisfying" day at school. Mercedes is my youngest child, but I have hope that one day she will have unbelievably satisfying days at school.

Section II

Creating College- and Career-Ready Learners

What Is a Learner?

In this section, I would like to explore what a college- and career-ready learner looks like. The list of essential questions in Figure II.1a forms the basis of the habits of mind that we seek to develop in college-ready learners.

What is a learner? A learner is a natural observer and mimic. From the time of birth to the age of two, a child is a learning prodigy. Think of what is learned during that time. We learn to manipulate and control our bodies to the extent that we can walk, move about, and run. We learn to recognize and respond to audio, visual, and sensory stimuli. We learn to use our senses (mainly our mouths) to explore and discover the world we live in. The most amazing thing we learn is how to communicate. Research shows that babies zero to eight months old, though they are not able to communicate effectively, are busy cataloguing language cues. By the time they are 11 months old, they recognize their native language from other languages and are able to differentiate the native sounds and ignore the non-native ones (Conboy *et al.*, 2008). For example, in English "ra" and "la" are different sounds because English uses a lot of r's and l's but in Japanese, these two sounds are identical because the Japanese don't really use either sound.[1]

If you want to see an amazing video, listen to Dr. Kuhl, from the University of Washington, describe how children learn languages from six to eight months old. Dr. Kuhl points out that "natural" language learning skills drop

Figure II.1   Habits of Mind at Central Park East Secondary School

Central Park East Secondary School's Habits of Mind, as Described by Deborah Meier in *The Power of Their Ideas*

♦ The question of evidence, or "How do we know what we know?"
♦ The question of viewpoint in all its multiplicity, or "Who's speaking?"
♦ The search for connection and patterns, or "What causes what?"
♦ Supposition, or "How might things have been different?"
♦ Why any of it matters, or "Who cares?"

Source: http://www.essentialschools.org/resources/521

off after seven years old. That doesn't mean we cannot learn other languages; it just means that our native language will get more and more in the way as we do. So, from birth, we are learning experts who learn by the observation and mimicry of the people in our lives.

What is a learner? A learner remembers what he or she learns. Could we say a learner is a "rememberer"? Yes, but that doesn't quite cover it, because I believe the learner wants to learn and not just remember. The act of learning is part of that desire. As we mature, we learn (and remember what we learn) more and more by exploration and discovery. We learn with hands-on and minds-on. We learn in the situation, in the moment, and in the locale. Unsurprisingly, this type of memory is called locale memory and is instant memory (Caine and Caine, 1991). For example, we all remember exactly what we were doing on our birthday. So we learn instantly by experiencing events that are important to us. What is a learner? A lover of stories. We (especially as children) love to listen to and tell stories. Daniel Willingham, a cognitive scientist and, as it turns out, a fellow Star Wars enthusiast, explains that we can easily remember complex storylines from movies or television shows that we have seen just one time (it really helps if the story is engaging, like Star Wars!) (2009, p. 51).

Using Star Wars[2] as a story example, Willingham goes on to describe the four C's that serve as a foundation for any worthy story: causality, conflict, complications, and character (see Figure II.2)—all held together by action (p. 52). So we easily learn content in the action and adventure of the story structure, all the while learning the facts and the complex concepts required for argument. What is a learner? A learner is a linguist capable of mimicking inflection, tone, and accent. A learner is a student in my class naturally copying the language of the teacher. As the teacher, I can tap into the student's natural ability and affinity to learn language by helping him or her learn the scientific vocabulary, capitalizing on the fact that the mouth is part of his or her natural language learning toolbox, directly connected to the brain. (There is no way students can remember a word if they can't say the word.) Spoken learning is powerful.

What is a learner? A learner is a problem solver, someone who can put all the learning and cognitive skills to use to find a solution. As her teacher, I can augment a student's inclination to learn by creating learning situations that require her to discover the reason pi equals 3.14 all by herself (this is inquiry). As her teacher, I can foment the incredible instant memory of stories by helping her think about the "meaning" by telling the story of Pearl Harbor using the four C's. As her teacher, I can provide opportunities to train her mouth as well as her brain. I can change the venue of learning, transform my classroom, or change the rules to create new locales for long-term learning. Most of all, I can inspire her to understand that the learner is the protagonist of learning, not merely the product of learning.

Figure II.2 The Four C's of a Story

Causality
Conflict
Complications
Character

Notes

1 They have a machine called an MEG (magnetoencephalography) which is different from CAT scans and MRIs. It is silent and does not require the subject to remain perfectly still, meaning it will not scare babies, and the subject can be awake while the testing is going on. There are other cool things about this machine, but the MEG opens up totally new horizons in learning how we learn. This is the link to the TED Talks video: https://www.ted.com/talks/patricia_kuhl_the_linguistic_genius_of_babies.

2 If you are interested in an amazing story, read *George Lucas: A Life* by Brian Jay Jones. Not only does it walk you through the successes and failures of George Lucas' life, it shines light on the thinking behind, and the success of, the Star Wars and Indiana Jones sagas. It also describes how George Lucas almost did not graduate from high school and his passion for improving the education system. As a result, he created the George Lucas Educational Foundation and Edutopia.org, the premier online clearing house for best practices in teaching and learning using hands-on, project-based learning. You can find me there as a blogger.

References

Caine, R. N., and Caine, G. (1991). *Teaching and the Human Brain*. Alexandria, VA: Association for Supervision and Curriculum Development.

Conboy, B. T., Sommerville, J. A., and Kuhl, P. K. (2008). Cognitive Control Factors in Speech Perception at 11 Months. *Developmental Psychology*, 44(5), 1505–12. doi:10.1037/a0012975.

Jones, B. J. (2016). *George Lucas: A Life*. New York, NY: Little, Brown and Company.

Willingham, D. (2010). *Why Don't Students Like School? A Cognitive Scientist Answers Questions about How the Mind Works and What It Means for Schools*. San Francisco, CA: Jossey-Bass.

Chapter 4

Inquisitive Learners

*Inquisitiveness: Curiosity about Surroundings,
Constantly Asking Questions: Why? How?*

Why Should Students Have an Inquisitive Nature?

One day, I walked into a Walgreens store looking to refill a prescription. Of course, they put the pharmacy way in the back so that unsuspecting customers looking to fill prescriptions or find medicine have to walk by all the other items that are enticingly displayed along the way. I was walking down one of those aisles and caught a glimpse of a Mason jar with a butterfly in it. The packaging of the jar pointed to a button that was labeled "Press Here." So I did. The plastic-winged butterfly began to flutter as if it had just been caught, and then settled down, slowly opening and closing its wings—just like a real butterfly would do. Did I just walk away and say, "That's cute"? Nope, I was curious how the butterfly was made to work that way. So I looked more closely to analyze the mechanism as I pushed the "Press Here" button several times. (This, by the way, is why you never want to select the first item in the pile to buy.) I found out that it is quite an ingenious device, based on a simple principle. Are you curious as to how it works?[1]

Much emphasis is placed on English language arts and mathematics. Some might say, "What about science and history?" Let's start with history. In order to interact with the content of history, what options do students have? They can talk to someone who has lived history, they can watch a movie about history, they can read about history, they can speak about history, and they can write about history. All of these activities require literacy skills. Without the effective literacy skills students would not be able to interact with history at the college and career level. The same learning characteristics we have already discussed with analytical thinking, critical thinking, and problem solving apply to literacy in any content area, including history. Now let's consider science. The bottom line for a scientist is to be inquisitive about things, to perform experiments, and to discover things. Well, that is the simplified version of science, but just like history, students must be adept at reading, writing, and conversing about science. Much of scientific research begins in the library, first understanding the achievements and discoveries of others and then finding out what needs more substantiation and what is still unknown. English language arts are therefore the foundation of scientific learning and understanding, hence the literacy foundation in all college- and career-readiness programs.

Isn't science in its own category in terms of learning? Not necessarily. We often hear of math and science sort of lumped together, but this may be because the two are challenging and difficult subjects for many people. Science learning depends on math learning, but not necessarily the other way around. A teacher quality program at Texas State University called Mix It Up[2] is trying to help teachers connect math and science conceptually and pedagogically. The premise is that public school science teachers understand the hands-on methods of laboratory experiments, but may be a little shaky on the math concepts, while math teachers teach mathematical procedures but might need help in making the math relevant. This is where the Mix-it-up program sees its opportunity. Dr. Sandra Moody-West and her team bring math and science teachers together and have them learn advanced math and science concepts conceptually. Then the two have to prepare and teach a correlated math and science lesson. Through this practice, Dr. Moody-West has seen math teachers integrate their learning activities with science teachers in the participating schools, and as a result, student understanding of math and science has increased. Dr. Moody-West, who is a biologist, will tell you that teaching science and math requires a lot of knowledge of English language arts.

How to Help Students Develop an Inquisitive Nature

Having an inquisitive nature was one of the characteristics of a college- or career-ready student, according to 400 university professors in Dr. Conley's 2003 landmark study. Higher education encourages curiosity, much more than EC–12 public education—except for perhaps Montessori schools—but public school children need it just as much as college students, if not more, because they have more to learn. Luckily, as discussed earlier, children are naturally curious and it follows that students should be also. I have never seen a student who was not curious about something. While I have seen a few students who have suppressed their curiosity when they enter school to such an extent as to be nearly undetectable, their curiosity is still there—which means that given the right circumstances, it can be revived. Human beings are hard-wired to be curious from birth, and being curious is a major activity of childhood and young adulthood (and yet recently, more and more students would rather be curious-looking, as evidenced by popular clothing styles). So if we notice students are not as curious in our classes as they should be, then we should first look at what we are doing, or not doing, that might cause this to happen. Of course, I have some suggestions of places to inspect first (see Figure 4.1). If the answer to any of the questions is no, then getting students to be curious again is a relatively easy fix—just change what we are doing or not doing. If all of the answers are yes, then the fix is still possible, but we have to be more patient. One of the foundational instructional methods for inciting curiosity is called inquiry. I need to caution you before we go further into inquiry.

The first caution is that inquiry is ideal for situations that can be discovered and explored. A science teacher would never use inquiry as an instructional

Figure 4.1   Conditions Necessary to Foment Curiosity

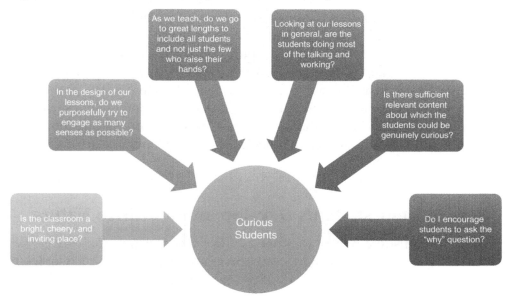

method to teach students safety. The best method for teaching lab safety is direct instruction (Madeline Hunter's [1994] seven-step lesson plan for example). The second caution is that in trying to get students to participate fully in the inquiry process, we have to remember that most likely, they have been conditioned to do the opposite of inquiry—shut up and listen. Depending on the severity of the case, it may take a while to get them "unconditioned." As an example of this, several years ago, I was involved with the Ford PAS[3] program, which has an awesome business/STEM inquiry-based curriculum. We brought in thirty ninth graders, from three different schools, for a nine-week summer course. The first week that students were presented with the inquiry lessons they did not know what to do. They just sat there silently. The Ford PAS folks had anticipated this and created a course to help students learn how to do inquiry. Since the summer program instructors had the students all day long, for the first week they used this introductory lesson and basically trained students how to ask questions, brainstorm solutions, collaborate with their groups, and investigate possibilities. You would not have recognized the groups after nine weeks. No one had to tell them to ask clarifying questions, critically analyze, or research; it was automatic. And instead of silence, an energetic buzz of conversation abounded when they were given their final assignment.

My point in sharing this is that if you are just starting inquiry, and have all of your other teaching ducks in order, then just be patient and for heaven's sake, don't freak out because of "silence" in the first inquiry lesson. You have to be willing to let students fail a few times before they get it. Students are smart, and they will remember what it is like to be intellectually curious, and they will appreciate the liberty that you are giving them. The most important thing about inquiry is that the learning scenario you set up must be compelling enough for students to become engaged.

You may object by saying, "But I don't have time to play games or do projects (or allow students to be curious). I have to teach them (drill them) on the content of the state standardized tests!"

I may quip, "So … ? Why is that your problem? The students are the ones who have to take the test; let them worry about it."

You may counter, "You don't get it. I am judged by how well my students perform on these state tests.[4] I seriously don't have time to do the fun stuff."

I most likely will reply sarcastically, "OK, I get it. You are graded on how well your students perform, but you are not interested in saving time in the long run and being a more effective teacher by helping your students be engaged in their own learning?"

With all of this pressure on students to perform well on standardized tests, we must understand that it is in our best interest to help students reignite their curiosity and interest in learning. We have to agree that the so-called higher-order "fun stuff" is not just fluff that can be discarded for lack of time; it is at the very core of how and why we learn at all. In the final analysis, the "fun stuff" will make teaching and learning easier and more enjoyable for everybody, and as a direct result of this, your students will remember more! As mentioned earlier, Dr. Willingham gets to the crux of the matter right away: It is not the state testing that is doing the damage to "education." It is the teacher's reflexive response to state testing that is causing the problem. Too many teachers assume that the best and quickest way to get information into students' brains is to tell them what they should know and then expect them to know it. Dr. Willingham introduces the concept that "Memory is the residue of thought" (p. 41). This means that we remember most what we think about most. If the students are interested and inspired to think about things for prolonged periods, then memory is enhanced. This is where inquiry, constructivism, and curiosity come into play; providing opportunities for students to think about what they are learning. In this way, memory is improved, students do better on standardized tests, and ... guess what? Students enjoy learning! Problem solved.

Memory is the residue of thought.

(WILLINGHAM)

S T R A T E G Y

Anticipatory Set[5]

The success of a lesson has much to do with the way it starts. Madeline Hunter knew this when she created the seven-step direct instruction lesson plan. The very first step is what she termed the Anticipatory Set (see Figure 4.2). Others may call it the "hook" or the introduction to the lesson. With students as sophisticated as they are, the anticipatory set has to be more than simply telling students what lesson is about. At the beginning of a lesson, teachers have a few critical moments when students' natural curiosity overpowers other interests.

Lessons should start off with something that grabs students' attention and doesn't let it go for 55 minutes. The anticipatory set also has another function. It firmly puts the teacher in the driver's seat (after all, it is a direct teach model) and reinforces the concept that the teacher has something urgent that students want. Let's approach the anticipatory set from a literature point of view. Much as a good story teller fabricates a new world with words, the teacher must set the learning stage before the main action, climax, and ultimate dénouement (I had to look this word up—it means unraveling of the plot) of the lesson can occur. (You recall that Willingham suggested that every lesson be told as a story in order for the students to have instant recall.) As teachers, you have two possible objectives of anticipatory sets: An introduction setting the stage for a lesson and building a conceptual framework into which the new learning of the lesson can be placed, or the expansion, review, or scaffolding of previously learned content. One of the exciting things about teaching and learning is that every day there are brand new opportunities to teach and learn that no amount of planning can anticipate, but having the anticipatory set helps the lesson get off on the right foot. A creative teacher can easily prepare lessons with something stunning and new to surprise or even shock students into alertness in the anticipatory set. The more you do this, the more firmly you establish a routine. Students (as well as teachers) are creatures of habits, and behavioristic conditioning works. If you have something interesting at the beginning of each class period, students will begin to expect it, and they will adjust their behavior to take advantage of it. I hope that the following techniques will give you some ideas for keeping students on their toes.

Figure 4.2 Two Purposes of the Anticipatory Set

TECHNIQUE: Sponge. The sponge is a tried-and-true instructional strategy that serves multiple purposes. It is called a sponge because it soaks up the wasted time at the beginning of a class while the teacher takes roll or passes back papers. Some call it a bell-ringer; others may call it the warm-up, flashback, or lesson opener. The most useful purpose is to get students busy and productive while the teacher takes care of attendance and getting the lesson started. It also sends a message to the students that their time is valuable enough for the teacher to not waste any of it. It establishes a sense of urgency and importance of the learning work done in the classroom, and it diminishes downtime that can allow behavior issues to arise. Just like the anticipatory set, it can serve as a review of prior material, or it can set the stage for learning new material. It must be something that students can perform independently, without the aid of the teacher (remember the teacher is busy taking roll, accepting and recording homework, counting school lunches, etc.).

The first five minutes of class is a perfect time to give pretests before a new concept is taught, or a short quiz to reinforce recall of important facts. The sponge activity needs to be something that students do not need the teacher to help them to do, because the teacher will be busy taking attendance, doing a lunch count, etc. Also, the sponge activity needs to be ready to go before students begin arriving in class. As students walk in, their eyes will be drawn to the whiteboard, overhead, chalkboard, or other display where they will have their independent work instructions for the next five minutes. It is important to set a time limit and stick to it (no more than five minutes). Then, to establish that the sponge is valuable learning, connect the sponge to the lesson at hand. For example, in chapter one, I shared with you that as a Spanish language teacher, I used Spanish sayings called *dichos* to help my students think abstractly, to learn about their culture, and to interact with the words in Spanish. As they came into class they wrote down the *dicho* in their journals, and in English gave an application of the *dicho*, while I took roll and checked homework. I just brainstormed for a few minutes and came up with several viable bellringer activities that I have listed below. Use them, modify them, or create your own.

- Science: *Term Boggle* (create as many science vocabulary words as possible from jumbled letters).
- Science: *Identify the Missing Step* (display a scientific process with a step missing); *Categories*. Place the jumbled word cards in the right categories.
- ELA: *Literary Terms.* Either provide a list of literary terms, or example sentences using those literary terms, or both. Students can do the following for review: match the terms with the sentences, categorize the sentences according to the literary terms, define the literary terms, provide their own examples of literary terms, or create a table of juxtaposed terms and determine what sentences might fit in the boxes (see Figure 4.3).

Figure 4.3   Decision Matrix for Literary Terms

	Foreshadow	Dénouement
Climax		
Conflict		

Jeff sliced the dragon open, and out came the not-so-beautiful but immensely relieved princess.

Senator Cruz rose to the platform, but before he could testify, the speaker of the house denied him the opportunity with the smash of the gavel.

Alice finally understood what the Cheshire cat was trying to tell her: If you do not know where you want to go, then anywhere is good enough.

	Foreshadow	Dénouement
Climax	Luke...	Alice ...
Conflict	The Wart..., Jeff...	Senator Cruz ...

Luke entered the cave and fought Darth Vader and with a swipe of his light saber cut off his head, but when it thudded on the ground, the face looking up at him was his own.

The Wart suffered abuse from Kay and Sir Ector in the form of hard labor, verbal slights, and neglect.

♦ Math: *Fix It.* Show problems worked out with one error, e.g., copied the wrong numbers or operations, misused the properties of equality, did the wrong calculation, or switched digits.

♦ Math: *Logic Buddies.* Pair the problems that use the same math operations, or process, for example 5[3x–2] would be paired with [16y–2][3y + 5] because both require the use of the distributive property).

♦ Social Studies: *Timeline.* Students are given a list of historical events with no dates and they must create a timeline, or fill the gaps on an incomplete timeline.

♦ Social Studies: *Dual Timeline.* Students compare two different topics in the same time period by filling in the timeline on the portion above the line with one topic and then underneath the line is filled with a different topic, e.g., on the top the students list the scientific breakthroughs in a time period, and on the bottom they list the political events that occurred at the same time. Try having students do a personal timeline with what they are learning on top and significant life events (achievements or challenges) on the bottom.[6]

S T R A T E G Y

Inquiry Learning

Inquiry learning is just that: students asking questions about something they do not know. Some obvious preparations must be made before inquiry learning is employed as a strategy. First, as mentioned earlier, not every lesson can be an inquiry lesson. For example, you do not want students exploring and experimenting with equipment for which they have not had safety training. The safety training would be provided in a "direct" instruction format. Additionally, in mathematics for example, before students can inquire about a mathematical situation, they need to know how to perform the operations. It is unlikely that students will come up with the algebraic theorems of equality on their own; therefore, to save time and frustration, students should be given the theorems and helped to learn them. After that, you can use inquiry to have students devise their own methods for converting inches to millimeters.

The Five E Learning Cycle.[7] This was designed primarily for inquiry use in science, but it also has been applied in other disciplines. The Five E Learning Cycle consists of the following phases: Engage, Explore, Explain, Evaluate, and Enhance. The key to inquiry is that it is the students doing the inquiry, not the teacher. The role of the teacher is to "prime the pump" as necessary to keep the inquiry going and on track, but students are the ones doing the heavy lifting. The teacher's main work in inquiry learning is creating and designing a learning environment that facilitates the discoveries.

TECHNIQUE: *Five Es. The first E is Engage.* The teacher might have to start the inquiry process off with an anticipatory set to get students asking questions, but once students are engaged, the teacher steps back into the facilitator role. For example, the teacher can start by showing a horrific explosion of a car set aflame by the Torch in the second *X-Men* movie. The car jumps in the air and then spins on its axis horizontally. Then the teacher shows a clip of how the explosion was created using scientific principles (transfer of energy from a rapidly spinning fly wheel to the car).[8] The teacher then shows students the bicycle wheels, the Lazy Susans, swivel chairs, gyroscopes, and other centripetal force devices for the Explore phase. Students are given 15 minutes to explore. The Explain phase will be the students either writing in their journals or sharing with their partners how spinning objects work and react to different forces. Then in the Evaluate phase, students are given the task of traveling from one location to another, balancing on a frame containing two gyroscopes, wait … that's riding a bike. Hmm … okay, how about this one … Students have to make a top that will spin for the longest amount of time possible using what they have learned. The Expand phase consists of students brainstorming about applications for the scientific principles they have learned, such as guidance devices on missiles, Segways®,[9] space vehicles, boats, submarines, hovercraft, etc.

S T R A T E G Y

Socratic Questioning

Socrates had the annoying habit of answering his students' questions with more questions. Bite your tongue and quit telling students what they should think. Making them come up with something is probably the first strategy that should guide all of our teaching. We do them no favors by just giving them the answers, especially when they don't even ask for them. Students remember the answers they come up with themselves and feel more satisfaction. The Socratic method is the basis of the AVID tutoring program. Two days every week, AVID students in their AVID elective class sit in groups of seven students and one college student acting as a tutor. The students must prepare their own questions and help each other arrive at solutions. The tutor will monitor the conversations, intercede only when necessary, but mostly ask probing questions designed to help students arrive at their own answers.

TECHNIQUE: Socratic Circles. The College Board's Advanced Placement program teacher training and the AVID teaching training both include the strategy of Socratic Circles.[10] The concept is that you have an inner circle of student experts who have read and studied a text. An outer circle of student observers watches as the teacher and students ask the inner circle questions about the text.

The teacher must have prepared a list of critical thinking questions rather than fact-based questions because it is nearly impossible to come up with Higher-Order Thinking Skills (HOTS) questions on the fly. This process is great for students who are beginners at critical questioning and who need to spend time observing both the teacher asking questions and the students in the middle answering them. A variation of this is that you eliminate the teacher involvement and assign the students observing to be the ones asking the HOTS questions either in turn or in a creative, random way.

TECHNIQUE: Answer a question with a question. When a student asks a question, the teacher has a variety of questions that can be asked back to help the student: Questions that seek clarification, questions that probe assumptions, questions that ask for reasons and evidence. For example, an elementary teacher may ask questions like the following:

♦ Questions that seek clarification: What do you mean by saying the sunfish looks like a pancake?
♦ Questions that probe assumptions: What does the shape of the sunfish have to do with its name?
♦ Questions that ask for reasons and evidence: Why doesn't the sunfish look like other fishes?

TECHNIQUE: Costa's Questions. Students understand more than we give them credit for. (This is a can of worms that some teachers may not want to open, but I think it is for the best.) As teachers, we should be using pre-prepared questions that cause students to think deeply and critically. Arthur Costa (2011) has simplified the six (or seven levels) of cognitive difficulty defined by Benjamin Bloom. Costa has only three levels of questioning:

1. Easy: knowledge-level comprehension questions;
2. Medium: analysis-level questions;
3. Challenging: questions that involve application, synthesis, and evaluation.

Teach students the three levels and show them how to identify which level of question is being asked by identifying questions in the textbook. Prepare students to spiral questions for each other by starting with level-one questions, then going to level-two questions, and finally going to level-three questions.

After training the students on Costa's levels of questions, the students are given five minutes to prepare three levels of questions to ask each other in groups of four on a predetermined topic. The students are given numbers, one through four, and then all the fours get together and ask each other their questions. Students have five minutes to practice classifying each question as they answer it. Then the competition begins. Students return to their own groups and in a *Jeopardy*-style game, the teacher gives the answer and each group of students is given an opportunity to either earn 10 points with a level-one question, 20 points with a level-two question, or 30 points for a level-three question.

Depending on how trusting of a teacher you are, you might allow students to judge your questions on a regular basis. Much like figure skating judges hold up numbered scores for performances, students can judge the level of the questions by holding up one finger, two fingers, or three fingers as you ask questions in the classroom.

Notes

1   I don't think they make them anymore, but you can still buy them on Amazon and Ebay. To satisfy your curiosity on how they work, go to this website: https://www.youtube.com/watch?v=9DyTx0hvmqE.
2   Take a look at Mix-it-up at Texas State University in San Marcos: http://www.bio.txstate.edu/seminars-and-events/Mix-it-up-Website.html and check out the WordPress® site at https://mixitupwebsite.wordpress.com/.
3   PAS stands for Partnerships for Advanced Studies and encourages partnerships with local business and schools. This is a program for high school and middle school students that use an inquiry-based curriculum. It is a STEM/business and leadership oriented program funded by the Ford Motor Company Fund (not the Ford Foundation). www.fordpas.org.
4   Just so you understand where I come from, I believe that there are many things in the current educational system that need to be changed; however, state standardized testing is not one of them (not nationalized testing). Although we have a long way to go, at least the state standardized testing sets minimum standards for teachers to attain (notice I did not say students—once the students are accountable, then we will see great improvements). While I am grateful for minimum standards, the main hurdle now is to get teachers to quit teaching only to the minimum standards, and instead, to inspire learning beyond them. Hopefully this book is helping you do this.
5   Dr. Madeline Hunter established the most well-known and widely used template for direct instruction in the early 1980s, and it is still the foundation of direct instruction today. The seven steps are Anticipatory Set, Input, Modeling, Checking for Understanding, Guided Practice, Independent Practice, and Evaluation (a good template can be found at http://www.onetohio.org/library/Documents/Dr%20Madeline%20Hunter%20Article1.pdf). Make no mistake, direct instruction using the Hunter seven-step lesson plan is effective (Schmoker, 2011; Steward *et al.*, 2010). In fact, Dr. Michael Schmoker, in his book Focus, establishes that if teachers consistently used this tried-and-true method, tremendous progress would be made toward student achievement (2011).
6   One of the most intriguing and creative résumés I have seen is actually a timeline of the individual's work, interests, effort, and preparation, all represented graphically. See for yourself: http://design.spotcoolstuff.com/wp-content/uploads/2010/09/full-infograph-resume.jpg.

7 Researchers at the University of California, Berkeley set out to validate theories by Piaget (Learning by Equilibration) and Bruner (Learning by Discovery and Learning by Conditioning) by creating the Science Curriculum Improvement Study (SCIS) program, a K–6 science program in the early 1970s (see Thier, H., Karplus, R., Lawson, C., Knoll, R., and Montgomery, M. (1970). Science curriculum improvement study. Chicago, IL: Rand McNally). In the 1980s, the three phases Exploration, Invention, and Discovery were expanded to Engage, Explore, Explain, Evaluate, and Extend in the BSCS science programs. Professor Maryann Coe at Midwestern State University has provided a great explanation of the modern application of the Five E Learning Cycle at http://www.thesciren.org/wp-content/uploads/2015/12/5E_LearningCycleModel.pdf. Retrieved March 28th, 2017.

8 One of the most engaging learning presentations I have seen is Steve Wolf's "Science in the Movies." He came to my little school district and put on several shows for students and workshops for the teachers. Steve is a former stuntman and gives a presentation on how scientific principles are applied in the movies. He demonstrates the states of matter, Newton's Laws, simple machines, and kinetic energy as well as other common scientific principles that students of all ages are learning. To see how you can get him to come to your school, check out his website: www.scienceinthemovies.com.

9 My mother bought an all-terrain Segway and rides it all over the Arizona desert. Dad takes the dogs out for runs every morning with it. Isn't technology marvelous? My parents are in their 80s.

10 For a complete turn-key package on how to do Socratic Seminars see http://fmsavid.weebly.com/uploads/2/9/1/1/2911966/socratic_seminar_instructions_and_handouts.pdf.

References

Conley, D. T. (2003). *Understanding University Success: A Project of the Association of the American Universities and the Pew Charitable Trusts*. Eugene, OR; Center for Educational Policy Research.

Costa, A. (2011). *Costa's Levels of Inquiry*. Retrieved March 20th, 2012 from *www.fresno.k12.ca.us/divdept/sscience/.../CostaQuestioning.pdf*.

Hunter, M. (1994). *Enhancing Teaching*. New York, NY: Macmillan College Publishing Company.

Willingham, D. (2010). *Why Don't Students Like School: A Cognitive Scientist Answers Questions about How the Mind Works and What It Means for Schools*. San Francisco, CA: Jossey-Bass.

Opportunistic Learners

Opportunistic: Interest in Taking Advantage
of Learning Opportunities

Why Do Students Need to Be Opportunistic Learners?

I used to own some property in southern Texas, where I became acquainted with a certain plant called Greenbriar.[1] This is a plant that, if left unchecked, will overtake your property in months. It is very hardy and nearly impossible to kill because its roots spread underground and sprouts can appear anywhere. It turns out that the most effective way to deal with this plant is also the most natural way: with a goat. Goats love to eat the plant and actually look for new shoots to pop up. I would like to compare students to goats in terms of being opportunistic learners. I will also be comparing the learning process to how goats consume and process their food. Take special note of the words bolded and underlined and you will see a remarkable alignment. Goats are hardy quadrupeds that can be found all over the globe. When I was in high school, my mother thought it would be a good idea to get a goat so we could milk her (by "we" she meant me). My mother was always coming up with what we thought were crazy ideas, but we'll talk about those later. I need to tell you that goat's milk is very creamy and takes some getting used to. Anyway, we built a comfy pen out of wood and fed her hay and leftover veggies.

One day we heard the goat bleating in the front of the house (the pen was in the back). We looked in the pen and saw that the goat had eaten through the thin boards on one side of her pen, creating a getaway escape route.

She had gotten out so she could have access to the fresh green grass nearby. This experience got me thinking about goats, though. They are known to eat just about anything, even things that we would not think are edible, such as wood. Goats aren't like cows, who eat only the green grass. Goats will eat the green, the stems, and the roots. Goats will eat the bark off your trees, the shoes off your feet, and the shirt off your back (especially if it is red—remember Bill Grogan's goat?). You can't tie a goat up with rope; the goat will eat right through it. Speaking of a goat on a rope[2] … no, I'd better stay on target. Anyway, goats are pretty indiscriminate about what they eat. Even more than that, as my goat demonstrated, they are opportunistic about what they eat. There is a reason why we only see herds of goats roaming around in harsh, inhospitable climates in the Middle East. The goats are successful at finding things to eat that will sustain them in hard times. I should point out that in the next paragraphs, you will receive a biology lesson in the goat gastrointestinal process. But this should come as no surprise because you are already familiar with many of the words that will be used, though you use them in other contexts. Hmm. It is amazing how many words for the digestive process find their way into descriptions of the learning process. For your convenience and added emphasis, I will type the words in bold.

Like goats and their appetites, college- and career-ready students need to be opportunistic about what they learn. In order for students to be opportunistic about learning, they, like goats on the lookout for Greenbriar shoots, need to be hungry for learning opportunities. It is an attitude that creates a constant thirst for discovery, exploration, and learning. Please do not stop your students when you find them grazing in an encyclopedia or browsing in the library. Having an opportunistic learning attitude assumes you are an active learner rather than a passive learner. Now don't get offended, but most teaching that happens in public schools (including in today's student-centered schools) only requires students to be passive learners. Listening is a passive learning activity, like sitting in the shade; it takes no thinking, while reading is an active learning behavior, like grazing on nice green grass, which is different than simply eating because it implies that you are covering territory as you eat and that you are choosing what you want to eat. A student doesn't need to do anything to listen (and doesn't get much from listening either), but students have to engage many things in order to read, and that makes it more memorable. Of course, active listening is possible, and if students are really interested, they focus, but in general we do not train students to listen actively. We simply tell them, "Be quiet and pay attention!"

This is where the difference between goats and students makes the comparison difficult, so bear with me. Goats[3] have four stomachs to **digest** the food (stuff) they eat (like other ruminants): the *rumen*, the *reticulum*, the *oma-*

sum, and the *abomasum*. College- and career-ready students also must have the capacity to digest all sorts of knowledge and skills. The first of the four stomachs in a goat is called the *rumen*. This stomach gathers what the goat has **grazed** and then **swallowed**. It acts like a **fermentation** vat that breaks down the fibers. Periodically, goats will **regurgitate** (cough up) the stuff in the rumen and chew it again—this is called rumination or **chewing the cud**. College- and career-ready students need to allow information to ferment a bit as **enzymes** do their work, and then chew on (ruminate) the ideas again later. Rarely will any knowledge produce understanding or long-term memory the first time it is **ingested**. The second stomach of the goat is called the *reticulum* and looks like a honeycomb. This serves as a **filter** for indigestible stuff the goat may have consumed. Like goats, students need to filter their knowledge for validity and reliability of sources and **eliminate** the junk. Later we will talk about validating sources in student research, but for now, a bit of incredulity will go a long way.

The third stomach of the goat is called the *omasum* and is where the water is removed and the major part of the energy **nutrients** begin to be absorbed. As students think, ponder, and meditate on the possibilities of the new knowledge, the ideas are refined, and as a result **fuel** more investigation and thought. "OK, I know where you are going with this," you say, "and I don't like it!" Calm down—we are talking about the good that the food does to the goat's body (and students' minds), not the waste that is discarded. OK?

The final goat stomach is called the *abomasum* (ab-omasum, makes sense). This final stomach is much like our own stomachs and uses **caustic acid** (HCl) to break down food into nutrients the goat's body can digest. The nutrients are **absorbed** in the intestines. College- and career-ready students will be able to take the refined ideas and break them down using critical thinking as if it were acid to eliminate fallacies, falsehoods, and errors and arrive at the substantive knowledge. The knowledge is absorbed into the system, and then it can be said of students that they have "**assimilated**" the knowledge. So there you have it. College- and career-ready students are like goats because they both consume opportunistically and have a process to be able to absorb the nutritive substances gained from the browsing or grazing. Also, college- and career-ready students are like goats because they are hardy and only assimilate what does them good, and you know what happens with the rest.

I know, you are saying, "Woah. This is way too much information about goats!" I'm not quite done with this yet. I found so many parallels with goat behavior and student learning that I decided to map them out for you (see Figure 5.1). Then I categorized the digestive process into four learning phases (like stomachs) (see Figure 5.2).

Figure 5.1 Goat Behavior and Desired Student Learning Behaviors

How to Help Students Take Advantage of Learning Opportunities

Learning opportunities abound and are encountered in many diverse situations. The trick is getting students to notice them and then take the time and effort to investigate them. I watched as a magnificent new teacher unfolded the world to students in ways they had never seen. It was a beautiful spring morning in rural Texas. I was going to another campus and noticed a young teacher like a Pied Piper with her entourage of children following her eagerly. It drew my attention to the situation, and I surreptitiously followed them.

Figure 5.2   Ruminant Digestion and Learning Comparison

It was obvious that these students adored their teacher, not because she was pretty or nice, but because she loved learning and radiated it. I watched as the teacher stopped the class periodically and they huddled around some flower or interesting plant or bug that she found. She asked students why they thought the flower was there, what the bug might eat, and how the plant could move toward the sun. I believe she was a third-grade teacher.

I saw her balance on the curb as she walked, and 50 little feet followed. I witnessed her raise her arms gracefully like wings with each step and 50 wings sprouted behind her. The line of students zigzagged and hopped on one foot, then the other in perfect cadence with the teacher as they traveled to the gymnasium. No student had to be told to keep up, pay attention, or stay in line because the students were so focused on the teacher and what interesting thing she would find or do. It took only a few minutes extra, but the rewards for the students would last a lifetime. This teacher understood that the best way to get students to be opportunistic learners was to model how to do it herself.

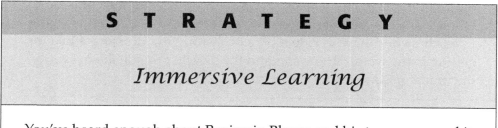

S T R A T E G Y

Immersive Learning

You've heard enough about Benjamin Bloom and his taxonomy, and it is well understood that we must work our way up it in order to more effectively cement knowledge or skills in students' memories. So let's suppose the foundation of "knowledge and understanding" a already done. As we discussed earlier, the main reason to use higher-order thinking skills (HOTS) is because students learn better (i.e., they remember or retain the knowledge and skills learned) when they are more fully engaged. In Bloom's terms, HOTS are defined as "application, analysis, synthesis, and evaluation" levels. You will recall that HOTS also engage the "Locale" memory system (so named by Caine and Caine, 1994)—instant memory, because they apply a learning opportunity to an experience and a location (locale). If we understand that no learning takes place independent of other learning then we have just defined a learning system, interconnected with other systems.[4]

Having established the above, then let me be the first to coin the phrase "HOTS Learning System." I can think of two instances in which we commonly create HOTS Learning Systems as parents: when our children are learning how to ride a bike or when they are learning how to swim. In the first case, we set them on the bike and start pushing them around until they get the hang of steering and stopping, and then we give them a big push and they do it on their own. In the swimming example, we get in the pool with them, and we let them get used to the water. We show them how to use their arms and feet. We get them used to putting their face in the water, and then we let them have at it. In both cases, we know they have learned the skill when they have achieved mastery … i.e., when they can ride the bike without crashing or they can successfully get around in the water.

Those are examples of HOTS Learning Systems. I call them systems because all the elements of the environment naturally promote the learning and provide immediate feedback through discovery, practice, and trial and error. The feedback then starts the learning cycle again. HOTS Learning Systems are self-sustaining and cyclical. Within these systems, both the bicycle and the water are essential elements, and they indiscriminately impose consequences for learning—or, for that matter, not learning. This new knowledge then affects the whole cycle. As an illustration of this model, can you imagine trying to teach a child how to ride a bike or swim without using a bike or getting in the water? The water and the bicycle provide the relevance, the urgent need to learn.

TECHNIQUE: *Creating HOTS Learning Systems.* The true magic, art, or science of being a professional educator is having the ability to create learning systems and, in essence, let them loose on students. We should be deliberate in designing our own classroom learning systems. Any true system must have a few elements, as shown in Figure 5.2. Because I have fond memories of many hours spent in the swimming pool both as a swimmer and a coach, I would like to illustrate this idea of learning systems using a pool as the classroom (see Figure 5.3). Although HOTS Learning Systems are most easily employed for more hands-on subjects such as the visual or performing arts, physical education, and the laboratory sciences, you can employ them effectively in any classroom.

♦ For example, a geometry class can set up a rubric for proofs that gives immediate feedback to students regarding their thinking when other students grade them. They then make the corrections and resubmit the proof.
♦ In an English class, the process of inner and outer circles establishes a system whereby students can discuss issues and delve more deeply into what they really mean (remember the Socratic Seminars we discussed earlier?). These are sometimes called inner and outer circles.

A creative teacher can make these resources available to students and can develop learning systems that automatically promote the kind of learning that engages students in HOTS.

Figure 5.3 Requirements for a HOTS Learning System

4. It must provide an opportunity for the learners to repeat the step until they get it right (which is the cyclical nature of systems).

1. It needs a personal learning goal.

2. It must have direct instruction, modeling, and guided practice in a realistic medium (thanks, Madeline Hunter).

3. It requires a performance method that demonstrates immediately the level of acquisition of knowledge or skills.

Figure 5.4 An Example of an Effective HOTS Learning System

4. The swimmer is naturally motivated by the relative success of being able to swim to some degree and not drown, and is therefore further encouraged to use those skills every time he or she gets in the pool.

1. In the pool, the personal goal is to navigate through the water successfully and not sink.

3. The performance method is the act of attempting to navigate the water. The level of learning is immediately apparent to both the parent and (especially) the struggling and gasping swimmer.

2. Direct instruction, modeling, and guided practice occur when the parent shows the child how to kick and pull the water to provide propulsion.

STRATEGY

Powers of Observation

Students notice all sorts of stuff about teachers, their classrooms, and their friends, but sometimes something might as well be invisible to them because it is so common, or it is so ubiquitous (I find pleasure in using that word, for some reason) that it is under the radar. I think of the "Jungle Book" song by Baloo as he is teaching Mowgli the necessities of life. He talks about turning over a rock and seeing the "fancy ants." Ants are everywhere, and most often we do not notice them because they are under rocks or out of view. When we get bit by one, then we notice. Observation is a skill that reveals what we do not know and as a matter of course what we can therefore learn once we realize it is there.

I am reminded of a story I heard in college about an aspiring young man who wished to be a scientist and learn at the hands of a particular scholar.[5] The first day, the eager young man arrived at the laboratory of the scholarly professor and asked him to start imparting his wisdom. The old man simply pulled off the shelf a dusty bottle filled with a little fish in alcohol. He set the large jar on the table and after explaining how to care for the jar said, "Tell me what you see."

Astounded at the easiness of the task, the young man responded, "This is nothing more than a fish in a bottle."

The old man shook his head wearily and said, "Keep looking." And then he walked out of the room.

This pattern was repeated for the next three days as the young man's frustration grew. After hours and hours of staring at the fish, the young man could not take it any longer. He decided he was going to talk to the professor in his office and inform him that he would be seeking another mentor. On the way, the young man struggled to reconcile the glowing praise that his comrades and the other professors had shared about this professor.

What was he supposed to learn from simply looking at a smelly fish? It occurred to the young man that he had not drawn the fish yet. So instead of going to the old professor's office, he went to the lab again, took down the old jar, and started looking for identifying marks on the fish. He carefully began drawing the fish and as he drew, he noticed unique and interesting details that he had overlooked in all his hours of staring at the fish. He looked closely at the scale patterns, the fin placement, and the other markings. The more he looked at this fish, the more he found that was unusual. After several hours, surrounded by his drawings, and other fish jars, the young man was still engrossed in the details of this little fish.

When the old professor came to look in on his pupil, he simply grinned, nodded his head, and matter-of-factly stated, "You are making progress. Keep looking."

TECHNIQUE: *Eiphen's Game:* [6] In the soon-to-be-published by yours truly, *The Amazing Adventures of Eiphen and the Orb*, Eiphen is a boy with incredible powers of observation. For example, he noticed that plants grow more at night than in the day. Eiphen observed that in order to fly as a vulture, he had to move his wings in a circular motion, not just up and down. He was the one who discovered the clue to opening the Wong Chinese puzzle box by noticing that one of the Chinese characters was sideways. Observation is not just looking at something, but also noticing something unique or different.

Eiphen's game helps students increase their powers of observation and their memory. It is a fun way to review for tests, do pre-reading preparation, or even introduce a new topic. The simple, non-technical form of the game requires the teacher to put no more than ten items on a table and cover them up with a cloth. All the students then gather around the table and as the teacher removes the cloth, the students have one minute to "observe" what is on the table. Then the teacher covers the items and instructs the students to sit and write everything they saw. In a "Boggle-style" fashion, students one-by-one call out the items they saw. If someone else saw the same item, they cross it off. The winner is the student or students who have correctly identified unique items. This helps vocabulary development because students need to know the names of the items they see. It involves non-linguistic representations because the items are things like buttons, keys, pencils, rulers, magnets, etc. Different versions of this game can be played using categories of items, such as things that come in sets of 12, or plants, or minerals, etc. Using the projector or smart board, vocabulary words, terms, graphics, charts, proofs, formula, equations, dates, concepts, or pictures can be displayed for a minute and then the same process can be used to report what they remember they observed. For more advanced students, you might show a set of words or pictures and ask the students to write down what things are missing from the set.

TECHNIQUE: Waldo's World. As children or with our own children, we loved to peruse the wacky pages of *Where's Waldo*, a series of books originally from England written by Martin Handford starting in 1987 (over there it is *Where's Wally*). The point of the books was to find Waldo amidst hundreds of similarly dressed people in red and white striped shirts and matching hats. The more distracting characters and the larger the number of drawings that were on the page, the harder it was to find Waldo.

This activity requires the teacher to prepare a target and a number of distractors that are similar to the target for which the students will search. For example, it could be a list of words that sound the same or similar like 1. red, 2. read, 3. Fred, 4. said, 5. dead, 6. led, 7. bed, 8. said. The teacher would then say one of the words in a sentence. "The mother read stories to her children every night." At the same time the teacher points to a picture of this sentence, or mimes the act of reading. The students then have to hold up the number of fingers that corresponds to the right answer. The topics can be more complex, a series of algebraic equations, chemical formulas, or famous people from history.

TECHNIQUE: Similarities and differences. Marzano et al.'s (2001) meta research on effective teaching strategies, including identifying similarities and differences, denotes this practice as having the largest average effect size (1.61 is considered huge) of the nine strategies they studied. This is astounding. Dr. Marzano and company in the second chapter of the book describe several techniques that can be used to help students identify and understand the similarities and differences. In their research, they identify four conclusions that help students learn from identifying similarities and differences: 1. The teacher can simply point out the similarities and differences. 2. The teacher can ask the students to identify the similarities and differences. 3. The teacher can ask the students to do a graphic organizer of the similarities and differences. 4. The teacher can ask the students to compare, classify, create metaphors, or create analogies. One technique that is not listed is the following: a prioritized list.

The teacher will ask the students to prioritize a list of characteristics or traits of several items or concepts. Students may now compare the lists and extract conclusions concerning the similarities and differences of the lists. For example, if students in the fourth grade are studying the properties of several liquids[7]—water, honey, dish soap, molasses, vegetable oil, rubbing alcohol, and corn syrup—students might create a prioritized list of qualities that best describe these liquids; honey might be sweet smell, yellow color, sticky (high viscosity), slow to pour, comes from animals, and heavy. When they get to corn syrup, which has a similar viscosity, their list might be slow to pour, sticky, heavy, clear color, comes from plants. They can identify that the major differences might be the clear color and the fact that corn syrup comes from plants. The savvy teacher will then ask the students to consider why the priorities are different. Then she can ask them to show what they have learned from comparisons and to ideate several conclusions regarding the differences in the liquids: 1) Liquids vary in weight due to density of the liquid. 2) Light liquids are also less sticky due to lower density. 3) Color and smell of the liquid are irrelevant to the other qualities. 4) Slipperiness may have something to do with the ability to dissolve other chemicals, etc.

S T R A T E G Y

Inductive and Deductive Reasoning

Dictionaries do not agree on what deductive and inductive reasoning are. Some say that deductive goes from general to specific and inductive from specific to general. Other dictionaries say that deduction establishes irrefutable facts, while induction deals only with most likely probabilities. Some definitions state that deduction deals with rules while induction deals with experiences. A deduced conclusion is not plainly stated but rather sits between facts. For our purposes, we will take deductive reasoning to mean concerned with concrete facts, and inductive to mean concerned with high degrees of probability. It really doesn't matter whether something is solved inductively or deductively, as long as it is solved. Both inductive and deductive thinking require that the facts be analyzed. Making the correct connections between the disparate facts makes solving the problem, as Holmes would put it, "elementary."

Figure 5.5 Example of Inference

The snow fell for three days, though after the first day it was not as thick and the wind quieted down. Sometimes Aaron felt that there could never have been a summer, that the snow had always fallen, ever since he could remember. He, Aaron, never had a father or mother or sisters. He was a snow child, born of the snow, and so was Zlateh. It was so quiet in the hay that his ears rang in the stillness. Aaron and Zlateh slept all night and a good part of the day. As for Aaron's dreams, they were all about warm weather. He dreamed of green fields, trees covered with blossoms, clear brooks, and singing birds. By the third night the snow had stopped, but Aaron did not dare to find his way home in the darkness. The sky became clear and the moon shone, casting silvery nets on the snow. Aaron dug his way out and looked at the world. It was all white, quiet, dreaming dreams of heavenly splendor. The stars were large and close. The moon swam in the sky as in a sea. Singer, Isaac Bashevis. "Zlateh the Goat." Zlateh the Goat and Other Stories. New York: HarperCollins, 2001.

TECHNIQUE: Inference. Provide for students a selection in which the situation must be inferred rather than explained. Have students work in pairs to deduce a conclusion from the relevant facts. An example is in Figure 5.5.

TECHNIQUE: Brainstorming with a twist. Brainstorming is best when it is done in groups of four or five students with the strict rule that no filtering is to occur. Okay, a little bit of filtering should be allowed for inappropriate words and topics, but other than that, everything is written down and accepted. The twist is added later. Change the location, change actors, change the perspective, or change the time frame. Students will have to filter their lists according to the twist.

For example, after having read Roald Dahl's (1983) book, *The Witches*, a fourth-grade class might start brainstorming about the topic, "If you are a witch, how could you hide who you really are?" Give students two minutes to write down everything they can think of (this works with individuals, pairs, or groups of four or five). The teacher then puts a twist on the thinking: "Which of your ideas would work when you are on the beach? When you are on a tennis court? When you are at Disneyland? Which ideas would you have to change? Any other ideas come to mind?"

TECHNIQUE: Solute versus solution. A solution is like water and sugar. Once they are mixed, they are not easily separated. They become a single unit. The solute is what is being dissolved, the sugar; the solvent is what does the dissolving, the water. Students' task is to identify the elements of the literature that are so intertwined as to be viewed as a single element, when in fact they are multiple elements. Shakespeare was a master at weaving different parts of his plays with different elements that seem to flow together. Perhaps the best example of this is *A Midsummer Night's Dream*, in which reality and surrealism exist seamlessly in the same space.

Ask the students to identify the elements of the play. Then have them discuss in pairs the following two questions: What is the solute in a *Midsummer Night's Dream*? What is the solvent? Have the students share the evidence for their mutual conclusions in a graphical organizer.

Notes

1 Greenbriar is one of the many varieties of *Smilax bona-nox*, of the lily family. It is a tuberous thorny vine that grows as much as three feet in one week and spreads through a system of underground roots that shoot up vines anywhere along the root. Just like Johnson grass, if any part of the root remains in the ground, the plant will still be able to grow. It climbs trees and if left unattended can create an almost impenetrable wall of tough, spikey vines.

2   Josh and Paul were walking through a field and saw a big hole. They wondered how deep it was, so they threw a rock in but didn't hear it hit the ground. They looked around and found a big log, which they dragged over and threw in the hole. Again, they didn't hear a thing, but all of a sudden a goat came running by at an incredible speed and dove down the hole. Still they didn't hear a sound. A bit later a farmer came by looking for his goat, and Josh said, "It might be the goat that just ran past and jumped in that big hole back there." "Oh, no," said the farmer, "that can't be ... my goat is tied to big heavy log."

3   If you would like to read more about goats and goat digestion, I found this Four H site rather helpful: www.ansci.cornell.edu/4H/meatgoats/meatgoatfs14.htm.

4   Yes, Systems Thinking is still alive and well. Peter Senge's book, *The Fifth Discipline: The Art and Practice of the Learning Organization*, was groundbreaking in 1990 when it was first published, so much so that it was republished in 2006. Senge makes the case that understanding systems will help any organization, including schools, learn to identify detrimental systems and replace them with productive systems. For example, the heating and cooling in our homes are a stasis system. It responds to data to keep the temperature in the home the same. Classroom instruction is a system. There are many types of systems. If you want to learn more about systems go to http://www.solonline.org/?page=PeterSenge or http://watersfoundation.org/.

5   This story actually happened and the process was repeated over and over on each new set of Harvard students. Now, it is told to aspiring students in colleges and universities worldwide to demonstrate the need for close observation and the corollary patience required. The professor in question is the famous Louis Agassiz, a renowned professor of ichthyology (the study of fish) at Harvard University (1848–1873). Two versions of this story can be traced back to two of his students: Samuel H. Scudder and Nathaniel Southgate Shaler. If you would like to read the real story written by Scudder instead of my watered-down summary, go to http://people.bethel.edu/~dhoward/resources/agassizfish/agassizfish.htm.

6   I have been writing a book ever since my own children were little. Obviously, it has to do with learning, but it is a fictional book about Eiphen, a boy who discovers an Orb from outer space and, with it, learns to enhance his imagination. He has several exciting adventures and has multitudes of puzzles to solve before he saves the world. http://eiphenandtheorb.yolasite.com/

7   Please note that if you want to use the same example of a liquids activity you should stay away from having students taste the liquids. Also for safety reasons, unless you have trained the students and have proper safety gear, stay away from caustic liquids such as bleach, vinegar, acids, and other cleaning fluids. For example, a common safety practice might be to measure viscosity by having the students use tongue depressors or rubber gloves.

References

Bloom B. S. (1956). *Taxonomy of Educational Objectives, Handbook I: The Cognitive Domain*. New York, NY: David McKay Co. Inc.

Caine, R. N. and Caine, G. (1991). *Teaching and the Human Brain*. Alexandria, VA: Association for Supervision and Curriculum Development.

Dahl, R. (1983). *The Witches*. New York, NY: Scholastic, Inc.

Handford, M. (1987). *Where's Waldo?* London, England: Walker Books.

Marzano, R., Pickering, D., and Pollock, J. (2001). *Classroom Instruction that Works:Research-based Strategies for Increasing Student Achievement*. Alexandria, VA: Association for Supervision and Curriculum Development.

Senge, P. (1990). *The Fifth Discipline: The Art and Practice of the Learning Organization*. New York, NY: Doubleday.

Singer, I. B. (2001). *Zlateh the Goat and Other Stories*. New York, NY: HarperCollins.

Flexible Learners

Flexibility: Ability and Desire to Cope with Frustration and Ambiguity

Why Do Students Need to Be Flexible Learners?

A while ago, I did an experiment with adult educators. I purposefully gave vague instructions on how to arrange groups with the hopes that they would figure it out. The goal was for each educator to participate in three different groups. I told them that the composition of each group had to be different. Their task was to get four different signatures from each of three groups listed on their worksheet. Everyone got one set of signatures right away. Getting the next set of signatures was more difficult because it had to be with different people. Some of the adults were willing to work it out, even using trial and error. Others would get to a point and realize that they did not understand what to do, and then would ask questions. A few began getting upset at the lack of directions and refused to try. I was hoping that the adults would be able to work together to negotiate the groups, but the project failed entirely. One adult asked me, "Why didn't you just ask us to count off by numbers and be done with it?" I learned that even adults have varying tolerances to ambiguity.

This example illustrates the fact that our students probably belong in one of these three groups: being comfortable with uncertainty, not being comfortable with uncertainty, and being irritated with uncertainty. In a 2011 study on student motivation, Kyndt *et al.* discovered that when students were given more autonomy, even though the amount of information or the level of uncertainty was the same, students perceived that there was less uncertainty and they were more apt to adopt a deep approach to learning rather than a superficial one. A certain amount of uncertainty cannot be avoided.

Uncertainty is messy, it is disorganized, it is unstructured, and it is organic. When doubt exists and the answer or path is not known beforehand, that is the essence of uncertainty. Apparently, according to the research, if students have to wait around for teachers to tell them what to do, the anxiety about uncertainty is raised, and students tend to go through the motions of learning as a result. But when students are internally motivated to learn, they are better able to cope with uncertainty, and they show resiliency in the face of not knowing precisely what to do next.

One of the main goals of secondary schools should be to prepare learners to be college- and career-ready by helping them deal with uncertainty and by helping them feel comfortable in postulating, guessing, hypothesizing, conjecturing, and testing their theories without knowing the answer and without knowing if there even is an answer. To our shame, in public education we have socialized students into believing that there is always a right answer and that the teacher is the guardian of that answer. We have misinformed students to such an extent that they believe that not being certain is a bad thing. As a result, few students are willing to take a risk and demonstrate their vulnerability. As I described earlier, the summer I spent with 30 Ford PAS students from inner-city schools in San Antonio showed me that in six weeks, this attitude can be turned around. Before I discuss how to do this, I want to make sure we understand what I am trying to communicate.

Helping students feel at ease with ambiguity does not mean that students remain blithely ignorant of the details or indifferent to the learning process. It means teachers provide students with the desire and the tools to deal effectively with ambiguous situations and provide a means to help them clarify the next steps. It means helping students confront uncertainty by identifying what is certain. It means helping students minimize the risks of getting the wrong answer and helping them feel confident that instead of having to choose the "correct answer," they can choose the best answer and support their decision with evidence. The purpose of this chapter is to provide a few ideas on how to help students develop strategies for dealing with uncertainty, ambiguity, and frustration.

Employing Uncertainty to Teach

Teachers need to inject a little uncertainty into their lessons every day because it engages students at the "analysis and above" levels commonly known as higher-order thinking skills (HOTS). This uncertainty forces students to evaluate what they know and do not know and to make a decision about it. Let's borrow an example from Steven R. Covey (1989), where he gives his audience a seemingly impossible task. He first fills a bucket with sand and asks an audience member to put all of the pebbles and larger rocks in the bucket. After several unsuccessful attempts, the participant gives up. Then Dr. Covey gives the participant a bucketful of rocks and tells the person to put in the pebbles and then the sand and water. Amazingly, it all fits. The message of prioritization provided by Dr. Covey's demonstration is not lost, but in this scenario, I am more interested in another message: when faced with the unknown, the improbable, or the impossible, a solution is discoverable if you have a strategy.

Thinking about sand and water, a math teacher could demonstrate the following problem: "Here we have a 100-ml beaker that is filled with sand and weighs 16 ounces. What is the volume of the sand?"

"100 millimeters!" the class responds.

"That is easy, right? Now let's magnify what we see in the beaker of sand."

The teacher holds up a beaker full of medium-sized rocks and asks, "If this represents the sand at high magnification, what do you notice about the volume?"

"There are gaps between the rocks."

"That is correct. Talk to your neighbor and come up with a way that you could you find the real volume of the sand. Discuss what other materials you would need and what math you would need to use to find the solution. You have five minutes."

This problem challenges students to think about what they know about volume and what assumptions they have made about the sand, mathematically and scientifically. Depending on students' age, various interesting activities can be done to investigate how the true volume of the sand can be measured. The simplest is to measure the amount of water needed until the sand is saturated and then subtract that from the graduated cylinder measurement.

In reality, the uncertainty principle is an inextricable part of math, statistics, and especially science, and as a matter of fact, it is accepted that any research involves a certain amount of uncertainty. There is no such thing as an exact science, so why would teaching and learning be any different? Students who feel confident in the face of uncertainty are better prepared to look at all the possibilities before choosing what they feel is the best answer. These students are less concerned about being told what to know and are more concerned with understanding why it should be known and how to know it.

How to Help Students Cope with Frustration and Ambiguity

Robotics competitions are full of frustration and ambiguity. Teams from all over the United States compete in the US FIRST® Robotics competition.[1] Each year, student teams are given a different task for their robots to complete. A typical competition includes a task similar to collecting basketballs and tossing them through the hoops. Students have to construct a robot that is no taller than seven feet and no wider than three feet (students have figured out how to unfold a taller and wider robot at the time of the competition, but they present the compact version at measurement time). The robotics team has to build the robot from scratch; no professionally designed kits can be used. The robot has to be able to move by radio control and on an autopilot program. It has to have mechanisms that can pick up the balls and toss them through hoops of different heights. And the robot has only two minutes and 15 seconds to accomplish the set task. The robot has to stay within boundaries of the competition area and garners fouls and penalties for breaking rules.

Given only these parameters, the students design a robot. They have to determine how the robot will move, what methods will be utilized to retrieve balls, and how they might get the robot to shoot them. They are given no designs, no direction, and no limits other than the size limits. They make their own conceptual drawings and then have to find out if the concept might work. They may make mini-robots to test their theories, or they might construct the individual mechanisms for testing independently. Once they complete all the testing, then they may be ready to build the full robot and then do more testing. Just think of all of the incredible learning opportunities this provides students!

By the time a team has made it to the national competition, they have already competed in local and regional ones, and most of the technology glitches have been worked out so they can focus more on strategies for dealing with the other competing robots and perfecting their robot-driving skills.

When I went to our local region with our fledgling team of robotics students for a simple LEGO® Mindstorms robotics competition, it was an eye-opening experience. Because this was our first time, my students were uncertain what the competition would be like. We also had a technical glitch that precipitated modifying the robot and the program just a few hours before the competition. This meant that the robot was still untested because certain parts of the program had to be rewritten due to the battery falling out when students arrived. During the competition, our robotics team discovered that not only were the robots to perform the tasks, but there was also a strategy of dealing with other robots that somehow our team had not considered.

Unfortunately, because of this surprise and first-time jitters, our team did not perform well (we didn't even get past the first round). In designing the robots, their biggest concern was the ability to perform the main functions of the competition. There were no guidelines, construction manuals, or directions on how to make your robot pick up a basketball and throw it, or in our case follow a printed line, grab thimbles, and drop them. The students simply had to figure it out on their own. This is uncertainty at a maximum level, but the students loved it!

In robotics competitions there are obvious ways to minimize the uncertainty: create detailed plans before you build the robot, test the parts independently before you assemble the robot, or build a smaller prototype robot and test it out before you build the big one. In the case of the larger competitions, the robotics teams have access to detailed dimensions and operations of the court, as well as actual videos of the court. These are important aids to reducing the ambiguity and uncertainty produced by these competitions. In the case of the smaller competitions in which we participated, the limited instructions were entirely written and did not provide an easy way of conceptualizing what would really happen. Our students did the best they could, but considerable frustration could have been eliminated with a few simple photographs of what the final product might look like. This has its dangers too; a photograph can be a limiting factor on creativity. It is entirely likely that if photographs had been provided, a large percentage of the robots would have been identical.

With that in mind, teachers need to be careful to identify the aims of any learning activity designed to help students deal with ambiguity, uncertainty, and frustration. There is nothing more frustrating to students than a teacher, who in the name of "building character," proposes that students engage in learning activities that have not been well thought out and prepared. In a student's mind, there is not much difference between a "complete waste of time" and "I want to see how you perform under stress." Inserting unknowns should be done on purpose and sparingly. Providing some answers or concreteness is primarily to help students focus on what is most important to learn rather than to have students waste valuable class time trying to figure out what to do. The idea of inquiry in boosting learning is best applied in small doses. Create learning environments—or what I call islands or bubbles of learning—within the limits of which students do not know the answers and must investigate and explore. Students must also be given a time limit and a rubric to gauge successful completion of the inquiry, otherwise the inquiry could take too much time and accomplish too little.

This reminds me of an immersive but sometimes frustrating video game that we purchased for my son when he was in high school. As it turns out, there is a series of this video game called the Elder Scrolls®[2] that came out in 2003, and my one and only experience with it began with a game called Morrowind®. It is a role-playing game that draws you in by not providing any information to start. The game begins by asking you what type of person you wish to be and what race. That is all you get. There is no help, no instructions, no idea of what you are to accomplish. Your new character has to investigate, observe, and ask the residents of the game a lot of questions. As you explore the Morrowind® virtual world, you discover a plot and what might be your role. This is an example of pure inquiry, but games like Morrowind® are not games that can be completed in days, weeks, or even months of playing. I logged many hours, and I still didn't come close to reaching the end. Anyway, the whole game is about finding out what you are about, and that is what inquiry is: going into a situation and not knowing what you will bring out. It takes some planning and some teacher trust to allow students to engage in inquiry learning, but the results are good for students and good for learning. With the addition of virtual reality goggles and cardboard head pieces, the idea of discovery learning is going to new levels. Some other interesting developments are occurring in interactive worlds such as Eduism for education and Second Life®.

There is a better way for students to learn, and at the heart of that improvement must be the students' active, willing, and even eager engagement in the learning process. When students are able to handle frustration and ambiguity, they are well on their way to becoming college- and career-ready. Following are some active learning strategies and techniques that will help students seek opportunities to learn.

S T R A T E G Y

Project-Based Learning

Another strategy is project-based learning, which is what the robotics programs really are. Given a problem, you have to come up with a solution or a product. Edutopia.org is a website that specializes in project-based design and contains many examples of projects developed by students and how to design them effectively. Unsurprisingly, it was created by George Lucas, who figured that there had to be a better way to teach students than the way he was taught in public schools.[3] Fortunately, the push for college and career readiness is perfectly in sync with George Lucas' vision of useful education.

TECHNIQUE: Simulations. When you go to the movies you are basically watching simulations of real life, dramatizations of what would happen or might happen in a distinct location or time. George Lucas is a master at re-creating those situations as demonstrated by his success as a director and producer of blockbuster movies. His genius stems from his understanding of what makes a good story. But, when you read his biography by Brian Jones (2016), what you learn is that at the beginning of George Lucas' career, coming up with the ideas for *Star Wars* was a lot of hard work and many revisions. We already know the power of storytelling in learning and we also know the importance of engaging students. If we combine those two elements what we end up with are simulations.

What simulations do for students is provide a reason to learn. In chapter five, I presented the HOTS Learning Systems. One required element of those systems is to provide a "performance method." This performance method is a way for the students to show what they have learned by putting it to use. This has a twofold benefit. Students have to remember what they have previously learned, and the act of applying it further pushes that learning into long-term memory, which of course is our goal.

As an example, in my Spanish language classes, since I want my students to be able to converse in Spanish, I have found it extremely useful to create simulations that promote this. In a small microcosm of an airport or a hotel, a lot of communication takes place and the students enjoy putting their skills to the test in these simulations.[4]

TECHNIQUE: Case studies. The first step in any research is to find out what has been done before. What have other researchers accomplished? What experiences did they have with this topic? Often research involves writing a case study about the researchers' learning experiences and documenting the educational journeys they have taken. Case studies are supposed to record what happened, good or bad. The researcher reflects on what happened and draws conclusions as to why it happened that way (Yin, 2009).

To set up a case study the students must have a question they want to have answered. It could be "What is the best way to sew a dress?", "How can I help my fellow students like writing essays?", "What is the best way to grow beans inside?", or "What is the best way to solve for the common denominator?" Then the students have to decide how they are going to get the information and experience they need to answer the question. It could be they have to just do it, or they have to interview someone. It could be they form a focus group. They take notes of their experience in a journal. Then they combine their notes and write a reflective summary of what happened. They look for patterns, ideas or experiences that are repeated.

They categorize and organize the gathered information in ways that make sense. Finally, the students draw conclusions from what their notes tell them.

TECHNIQUE: *Videography and documentation*. Most students have amazing cameras and video recorders attached to their phones. The typical uses for these marvelous tools are to Snapchat, Facebook, or Instagram a picture or video to get a laugh, or share an experience with friends (or strangers). What if students were actually given a task to do with that marvelous recording device? In cooperative learning usually one person is a recorder. Why not assign that person to videorecord the process and create a behind-the-scenes presentation of what happened in the group?

Here is another idea. Evernote (Evernote.com) is a free experience and idea recording app that will not only let students record written thoughts, but they can also include videos, pictures, and locations from multiple different sources and then puts it all together and coordinates with email to share what just occurred and collaborate with other students.

S T R A T E G Y

Prime the Pump. Here's the Main Idea—You Work Out the Details

The unique role of teacher and student in modern schools poses a conundrum. A teacher has knowledge and experience, and students need that. The problem is that a teacher cannot just give knowledge and skills to students. If he does, then students will not, and for the most part, cannot take advantage of them. In essence, the knowledge and skills offered will be wasted. In order for students to be able to really acquire, assimilate, and integrate the knowledge and skills, students must seek knowledge and skills for themselves and find them on their own terms. They must reinvent the wheel in order to appreciate it and improve upon it. The hardest part of this process for students is getting started. It is at this juncture that the best role of the teacher is to prime the pump and then get out of the way.

TECHNIQUE: *Magic wand*. Sometimes students are inhibited by reality and do not know where to begin in terms of projects. At these times, a teacher can change the situation by giving them a magic wand that can ignore reality. This wand can be selective or all-inclusive. You can creatively limit the power of the wand to drive the thinking in productive directions. For an example of a selective wand, you set up a learning scenario in which students must communicate with Martians, and the wand allows only the Martians to understand you, but you still cannot understand the Martian speech. "How can you get around this problem and still communicate effectively with the Martians?"[5]

TECHNIQUE: *Performance rubrics.* Simply writing down what students are to accomplish helps refine the standards of performance and diminish the ambiguity. When students know what kind and quality of product they must produce, they have a better idea of where to direct their search for learning opportunities. Below is an example of a simple performance rubric that will help students decide to do the best job possible on a history project about the Civil War (see Figure 6.1).

TECHNIQUE: *Finish it.* Much like the well-used technique of providing a writing stem or prompt for writing, the same can be done with mathematical proofs, solving equations, and working out word problems. Getting started on each of these is the hardest part. Once the teacher gives a clue as to the right direction, students are able to choose the next steps more effectively. For example, providing the first step in factoring the equation $x^2 - 6x + 9$ would be (x)(x). This would help the student know to use the FOIL (First, Outer, Inner, Last) method to find the correct binomial factors.

Figure 6.1   Sample Rubric for a Presentation on the Civil War

Unsuccessful Project	Successful Project (C grade)	Superior Project (A grade)
Students fail to visually represent three historical facts about the Civil War.	Students visually display three main historical facts about the Civil War in a poster, diorama, or PowerPoint presentation.	Students visually display three main historical facts about the Civil War in a video interview, interactive Hyperstudio, or Prezi presentation.
Students provide limited or inaccurate information for each fact.	Students provide explanations for each fact: dates, persons involved, locations.	Students provide explanations for each fact: dates, persons involved, locations.
Students fail to provide adequate historical context.	Students provide a historical context: What else was happening at that time?	Students provide three different influences that affected the outcome of the Civil War.
Students fail to adequately make connections among the facts.	Students explain how all the facts relate to each other.	Students engage the class in discovering how all the facts relate to each other.
Student presentation to the class is unprepared and poorly presented.	Students confidently present their information to the class.	Students engage the class in a short learning activity like a quiz show or competition.

S T R A T E G Y

The Future Is Uncertain

My son Gideon's favorite animated movie for a while was *Meet the Robinsons*.[6] Aside from having catchy music, the movie is appealing because the theme song has a good message, "The future is alive...." The main character, Robinson, learns that the key to a happy life is to "keep moving forward." For students, the future is nebulous because the only thing they can judge it by is the present. But they can keep moving forward. The value of projecting current behaviors into the future (trend analysis) gives students a coping mechanism for dealing with the uncertainty of the future.

TECHNIQUE: Plan ten years in the future. The perfect tool for this technique is the spreadsheet. Mathematics teachers can capitalize on the "Fill Series" command to help students create linear projections of the future. In the spreadsheet, students type in a beginning number, then highlight that number and nine cells below it. Once highlighted, students can either use the menu or shortcuts to define the "Step" or gap between numbers (i.e., for 1, 2, 3 ... the Step would be 1. For 2, 4, 6 ... the Step would be 2, and so on). Having chosen "1" as the initial number, if the Step is two, then the resulting numbers will be 1, 3, 5, 7 .... To perform geometric or exponential projections, students will need to know how to create and copy corresponding formulas into cells. The teacher can provide concrete examples of growth models: bacteria reproduction, simple versus compound interest, acceleration of free falling objects, etc. Students can begin comparing linear growth to geometric or exponential growth and predict their outcome after ten years. Students can represent the growth graphically (and creatively) in numerous ways. Another useful but slightly more advanced command is the "Goal Seek" command. Given a formula, students can select a target value that is derived from different elements in the formula. The program will automatically adjust those elements to arrive at the sought-after goal. This is particularly useful in situations where changing one variable also affects the other variable. "Goal Seek" is a balancing act that is much better suited for the computer to figure out. This is one of those cases in which it is better to give students the tool rather than have them try to figure it out on their own. With the "Goal

Seek" tool, students will be able to engage in predicting the future based on changing one variable in the equation.

TECHNIQUE: Prognostication. A gypsy fortune teller may look into a crystal ball, read Tarot cards, or examine the unique lines on your palms to predict your future. A true prognosticator uses more reliable sources to predict the future, but the process is pretty similar. Fantasy football, betting on horse races, and the stock market all require the participant to do some research, find out what has been the dominant pattern in the past, and then, based on current conditions, make an educated guess regarding the future outcomes.

In geometry, for example, given a certain initial scenario, a student must either prove it to be so or disprove it through a series of proofs. It helps to organize the information in terms of what is known or accepted as fact and what is not known. Then the geometry student must refer to learned information about relationships of geometric principles to construct an argument for or against the scenario. In other words, have the students guess what the outcome will be before they actually write the proof. Similarly, in English, students have already read the first chapter. The teacher gives them a prompt for prognosticating what will be the outcome of activities that took place in this chapter. The students can also predict what else may happen in the next chapter.

TECHNIQUE: Meteorologist—weatherman or -woman. Similar to a prognosticator, before any weather predictions can be made, the weatherman has to have a body of knowledge regarding how the weather typically behaves at the current time of the year and in the current locations. Unlike the prognosticators, the meteorologists can step outside, look at the sky, and say it going to rain (duh). Meteorologists must present their information— what is going to happen today, tomorrow, and the week forecast, the highs and lows, and warnings about severe weather.

Students can use the same pattern of presentation to share their predictions about economics, public opinion, chemical reactions, social issues, and of course the local weather.

Notes

1 FIRST® Robotic competitions began in 1992 in New Hampshire and have grown into a national competition involving almost 250,000 students. You might be interested to see video footage of past competitions at www.usfirst.org.

2   Bethesda Softworks released the first of the Elder Scroll series role play games in 1994 as an MSDOS game. Morrowind was marketed as an Xbox game in May of 2003 and is the third in the series. Two sequels followed Morrowind: Oblivion and Skyrim. Check out Morrowind online at http://www.elderscrollsonline.com/en-us/morrowind. Be careful, however, the sequels are like Morrowind, so be prepared to spend lots of time in the interesting and engaging worlds. They can become quite addictive. I wouldn't know by experience of course, so I am told … (wink, wink). Also, the MacIntosh Myst series of games was a precursor to this game, just as engaging, but the actions and physical awareness are much more limited.

3   The George Lucas Educational Foundation promotes evidence-based strategies that improve student learning in innovative and replicable ways. They emphasize project-based learning and technology integration in schools. Check them out at www.edutopia.org, and while you are there, you can check me out—I am one of their featured bloggers.

4   I wrote an article for Edutopia.org (founded by George Lucas, unsurprisingly) about the details of these simulations that can be found at https://www.edutopia.org/blog/creating-learning-environments-ben-johnson.

5   Amy Adams plays a linguistics professor, Louise Banks, in the movie *Arrival* (2016), which has a similar plot. Aliens land on Earth and are open to communication, but neither species is able to at first. Louise (is that an allusion to her *Superman* roles?) figures out that they can communicate with symbols, learns their writing style, and saves the world.

6   This is a 2007 Disney animated movie about an orphaned boy named Lewis, who is brought into his future to resolve an evil plot, and in the process meets his future family and learns a few things about himself. See http://movies.disney.com/meet-the-robinsons.

References

Covey, S. R. (1989). *The Seven Habits of Highly Effective People: Restoring the Character Ethic*. New York, NY: Simon and Schuster.

Kyndt, E., Dochy, F., Struyven, K., and Cascallar, E. (2011). The Direct and Indirect Effect of Motivation for Learning on Students' Approaches to Learning through the Perceptions of Workload and Task Complexity. *Higher Education Research & Development*, 30(2), 135–50. doi:10.1080/0729 4360.2010.501329.

Levine, D. (Producer), Villeneuve, D. (Director). (2016). *Arrival* [Motion Picture]. USA: 21 Laps Entertainment.

McKim, D. (Producer), Anderson, S. J. (Director). (2007). *Meet the Robinsons* [Motion Picture]. USA: Walt Disney Animation Studios.

Yin, R. K. (2009). *Case Study Research: Design and Methods*. Fourth Edition. Thousand Oaks, CA: Sage.

SECTION II
CONCLUSION

College- and Career-Ready Learners Feel a Sense of Urgency

What you believe as a teacher is the reality of your instruction. Everything you do as a teacher stems from what you value most. Students notice this, but have you noticed how much of an influence you, as a teacher, have on the way students feel about learning in your classroom? Your interests, your curiosity, and your skills can all find reflections in the eyes of your students. You are the model that your students aspire to become. We've all had days when we are on fire, students are excited, and everything seems to happen just the way we planned. Why can't we have those days every day? There are a multitude of reasons, but most of them are either related to or directly linked with what we as teachers do. Yes, there are always student issues, but we can anticipate those and compensate for them.

So if the teacher controls the mood and energy of the class, what feeling should you have to prepare students to be college- and career-ready when they leave your classroom? May I suggest a sense of urgency? (But not the restroom kind.) To get an idea of what urgency feels like, let's look at the story about the would-be student of a great teacher: the student pressed the teacher to tell him what he must do to gain great knowledge. After much badgering, the teacher finally told the pupil to meet him at the beach the next morning so he could answer his question. The next day, they met on the beach. The teacher walked into the water and motioned for the student to follow. When the student got close, the teacher grabbed him and pushed his head underwater, holding it there for a while. The student struggled, first because of his surprise and then because he needed air. Finally, the teacher let the student up, gasping for breath.

The teacher asked the student, "While you were underwater, what did you want more than anything else?"

"Breath!" was the ragged reply. The teacher explained, "If you want great knowledge, then you must want it as badly as you wanted to breathe."[1]

Do you have that sense of urgency in front of your students? Can you imagine getting your students to feel that level of urgency? It is possible if we establish a learning environment that promotes it. The very first factor is that we have to be on fire before we will kindle any fire in our students. We set the mood with our expressions, the way we walk, and the tone of our voice. We have to ask ourselves each class, "Am I urgent enough to inspire students to want to learn?" Often the kind of urgency we want in our students is intrinsic to the learning activity itself. Drawing out this powerful urgency means that our learning tasks have to be important and must require immediate attention. First, we must provide a reason to learn (which is analogous to sticking the student's head underwater). Second, we have to establish a need in our students to learn now (like a person whose head is underwater and needs to breathe). Here are my ideas for learning systems that promote urgency (see Figure II.3).

In order for learning activities to be most effective, you have to design them to be part of a learning system in which all the parts work together. If the teacher's behavior demonstrates a sense of urgency, students' behavior will most likely follow suit. Urgency is the spark of energy students need to engage in the difficult task of acquiring knowledge and skills. If applied correctly, the process of teaching and learning is efficient and fun. So when students enter your classroom, you want them to want to feel a sense of urgency. They need to want to learn what you have prepared as badly as they want to breathe.

In this section, we have discussed developing an inquisitive nature in each student, helping students to take advantage of learning opportunities, and strategies that will help students deal effectively with uncertainty and ambiguity. Combine all of that with an intense sense of urgency, meaning we have important things to learn right away, and students will be well on their way to becoming college- and career-ready.

Note

1 This story is attributed to Socrates teaching Plato, his student, a lesson. In that version, Socrates actually holds Plato under the water till he passes out.

Figure II.3 Learning Environments that Promote Urgency

Provide a Reason to Learn—Make It Relevant:

* Establish realistic products the students will create as a result of the desired learning.
* Bring in an expert who can give the students real-life problems they need to solve using the desired knowledge.
* Make connections with the other subjects the students are learning about.

Establish a Need to Do It Now—Make It Timebound:

* Set up time limits and follow up with consequences for not meeting them.
* Organize races and contests. (Check out an example of a math contest called Subtraction War, from Teachers.net.)
* Help the students set their own goals and timelines.

Make It Personal—Measure and Celebrate Success:

* Allow students to choose among different methods, not just levels of difficulty or depth.
* Give students an opportunity to present or publish their work outside of class.
* Prepare and administer pretests to which students can compare how much they have learned.

Section III

Building Resiliency

The Hard Work and Exhilaration of Learning Builds Resiliency

"Just two hundred more yards!" Flip, push off, breathe. Right, left, right, breathe. Left, right, left, breathe.

"Remember, long stroke, all the way forward and all the way back, deep." I can't get enough breath. Flip, push off, breathe … breathe again.

"You can do it, Ben!" My arms are complaining; the ache goes down to the fingertips.

"Only one hundred fifty left! Don't slow down." Kick more. Keep the rhythm: stroke, kick, stroke, kick, stroke, kick, breathe, repeat … flip, push off, breathe … big breath.

"Only fifty left. Pick it up! Pull harder, all the way forward and all the way back." Have to breathe every stroke. Gasp. Pulse is pounding, adrenaline kicks in … swimming faster, harder.

"Almost there!" Must keep swinging the arms even though they feel like lead: right, left, right ….

"Done!"

Rest, check pulse, float. Exhilaration!

I still like swimming, but when I was a youth, I swam the mile competitively (I was a scrawny kid and I had no muscle, but I could swim forever). I still swim, but now I prefer the longer distances. I recently set and met a goal to swim the mile without stopping. My wife calls me amazing, though others in the pool went much further and faster than I did. My colleagues just think I am crazy. Swimming the mile was hard work that required everything I had in order to complete it. I knew I could do it, but I had not really done it since I was in college 30 years ago. I did it because I knew it would be a milestone for me to get further in shape. I didn't worry about how long it took me; speed would come later. I met my goal to swim 1,650 yards freestyle without stopping, even though there were no cheering crowds or gold medals. My motivation was internal and self-perpetuating. I knew I was accomplishing a tremendous feat for myself, and that made all the difference. You have probably had similar experiences with training for marathons or other athletic competitions.

In this chapter, we will be investigating motivation and factors that contribute to developing it. Let me remind you and all of your students that learning is hard work, just like swimming a mile without stopping. Any coach can tell you that growth only comes when you stretch further than you think you can and practice more than you think you need to. When you read deeper, think longer, and create more enthusiastically, that is when the learning really happens. Then, when you help students admire their work, it is exhilarating for them to know that they have accomplished a challenging and difficult goal.

More likely than not, no one outside of your class will know how much they have learned, but you will know and they will know. There will be no cheering crowds and no fame or fortune. Nevertheless, because you have the data (pretest and post-test) on how much they have progressed, they will feel satisfied, complete … ready for more. Their motivation to learn more will be fueled just because they completed their challenging learning goal. Surprisingly, the hard work has not scared them off and their resolve and determination to succeed have not diminished. The eagerness for the next learning adventure wells up within them as they reach out for new knowledge and skills. This is when learning is fun!

Each student needs and deserves his or her own internal motivation to learn. In order for this to blossom within the students, some simple things need to happen. Teachers need to create an atmosphere of belonging to a high-performance learning team—learning is the goal and every learning activity (adventure) is designed to bring the students closer to that goal.

I have been privileged to witness teachers who have done these very things for their students, and I thank them for instilling this lifelong learning drive and thirst for knowledge in me. In this section, I will encourage you to teach students how to seek after and accept critical feedback, adjust to that feedback, face daunting tasks like swimming a mile, and develop the resiliency necessary to be active college- and career-ready learners (see Figure III.1).

Figure III.1 Eight Things Students Need in Order to Learn

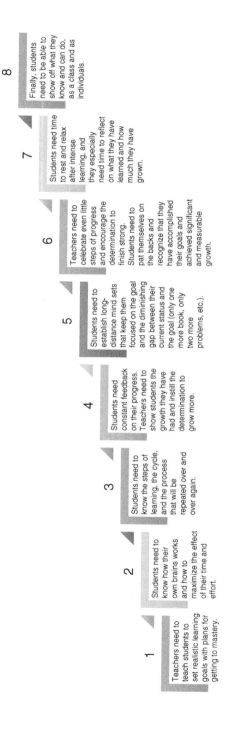

1

Teachers need to teach students to set realistic learning goals with plans for getting to mastery.

2

Students need to know how their own brains works and how to maximize the effect of their time and effort.

3

Students need to know the steps of learning, the cycle, and the process that will be repeated over and over again.

4

Students need constant feedback on their progress. Teachers need to show students the growth they have had and instill the determination to grow more.

5

Students need to establish long-distance mind sets that keep them focused on the goal and the diminishing gap between their current status and the goal (only one more book, only two more problems, etc.).

6

Teachers need to celebrate even little steps of progress and encourage the determination to finish strong. Students need to pat themselves on the backs and recognize that they have accomplished their goals and achieved significant and measurable growth.

7

Students need time to rest and relax after intense learning, and they especially need time to reflect on what they have learned and how much they have grown.

8

Finally, students need to be able to show off what they know and can do, as a class and as individuals.

Chapter 7

Willingness to Accept Critical Feedback

Accepting Critical Feedback:
Eagerness to Find Ways to Improve

Why Do Students Need to Be Able to Accept Critical Feedback?

How do you help students accept and even seek critical feedback in today's society where everyone is a winner? The entitlement attitude of "showing up gets me a trophy" is not going to work in the real world. So how do you get students to first of all accept critical feedback and, second, want it? Before I begin answering that question, it is important to make sure that we are on the same page in terms of what critical feedback means. Critical feedback is what happens when the results are compared to the expectations. Critical feedback implies that the goals were not met, but the most important part of that feedback is what was wrong and how to fix it. Students deserve to know when they did not meet the standards, what they got wrong, and how they can fix the problem.

Now this is where some educators start cringing. I said "problem" and "wrong" in the same sentence. We are not supposed to say such mean words. We must use words such as "areas of enhancement," not student problems. Believe it or not, most students appreciate it when they are told that their performance could have been better and are given specific ways that they can improve it. Perfection is unattainable in this life. Everyone can do better at everything. Teachers do no favor to a student by withholding negative feedback or padding it to such a degree that the student doesn't feel the need to improve. This is not to say once a student has reached mastery that you keep criticizing, but use the Big Mac approach (a criticism sandwiched between two compliments,) and it is easier to swallow. Students deserve to know the good and the bad (yes, I said bad) and even the ugly.[1] How are they supposed to know how to improve unless they are tested against a standard and receive continual feedback? After all, it is all about learning, right?

Another thing to consider is our learning plan. For example, when a student is given a learning assignment to turn in, is it really a "learning" assignment if they have only one chance at meeting the mastery level standard? How are they supposed to show that they have "learned" if they only get to do it once? Here is a suggestion. When a student submits a substandard piece of work, rather than assign a grade immediately, we can provide personalized, individual feedback to that student, including suggestions for improvement, and give it back to the student for revision! Is there a limit to the number of times this can be done to help a student overcome a particular learning obstacle? Some students might be able to do it right the first time, while others need several revisions. Typically, we see this kind of opportunity in English and social studies classes. It's called a "rough draft." Why not do the same in math and science? After all, if the student eventually gets the concept, isn't that what counts? The thing I like about the concept of assessing to provide feedback for improved performance the next time around is that no student is left out—not even the quiet, no-problem kids.

Using assessments as a learning tool is not necessarily a new topic. It is rare, but the concept has been around a while. I would like to revisit it with a personal analogy. I took the Cisco Networking Class one summer, and we completed a whole semester of a high school course in one week.[2] We spent two hours listening to a lecture of the key points and then we took a test. In order to continue the program, we had to pass the test with an 85 percent. Talk about high stakes! When I was taking the tests, I noticed something. Since we studied the chapter the night before (supposedly), and since we just went over the material, you would think the tests would have been easy, but some of the questions were designed to trick us into selecting the wrong answer. So even though I was well versed in the material and it was fresh in my mind, I never aced any of the tests. (Grrr!) I passed them—most reasonably well and some just barely—but it was frustrating not to do perfectly. The fact that others were struggling too helped assuage my pride, but the one student in the class who got 100 percent got open congratulations from all of us and … at least from me, he got a silent, "I'll catch you yet!"

Anyway, this got me thinking. If we want to test a student's knowledge, shouldn't we just straight out ask the question? Is it necessary to throw in distracters, misleading answers, and ones that are close to the right answer but not quite? Is that fair? Hold that thought. When I was taking the "Assessment Design" class in college as I prepared to become a teacher, I remember saying to myself, "What teacher is going to have time to make all of these test questions and design a scientific pretest and posttest for every unit?" I have since discovered the answer to that question. I know that I did not make or take the time to make such elaborate quizzes or tests, and from my personal experience, neither do many other teachers. Another question then: If valid assessment is so important, how do you do this? Before I answer that, let's go back to my other thought.

Distracters, misleading answers, and trick questions are important for establishing level of difficulty; we can't get rid of them! Since we have to differentiate our instruction, why not our tests too? The same students who have different learning needs are the same ones taking the tests. Another reason is that there are two types of tests, summative and formative. One of the safety nets of my Cisco class is that our instructor gives us three chances to take the test. After taking each test, we can look at the right answers and figure out what we did wrong and then take the test again. This is the main characteristic of formative tests—a chance to take it again. But when I go back and figure out how I blew the question, I actually learn better. It sticks in my brain better!

Back in my college assessment design class, I learned that each test needs to have some easy questions, some challenging questions, and some hard questions. A sophisticated teacher will assign different point values for each. A more sophisticated teacher will make sure that each question is also aligned with a state standard (but that is a conversation for another day). Anyway, the struggling student will most likely get the easy questions, while the advanced student will be challenged with the hard ones. Both will feel that the test has made them stretch, and both can feel success in the questions answered correctly.

How can we find time for this? The way to find time is simple. You work with your teacher peers and come up with the pre- and posttests together (unless you teach in a small school where you are the only teacher and are willing to give up your summer vacation to redo all of your tests by mining the textbooks and the Internet). You share ideas, and you design a better mouse trap ... I mean you design a better test, as a group. Now if you consider the sophistication I've mentioned, you all will be able to gather valuable student information that helps you compare teaching performance ... and predict student performance on state testing. Some other time-saving tools are question item banks, scanners, and online test-taking tools. If developed together, the test will be a better product, and it will be more useful, more productive, and less time-consuming for the teacher. We can't expect students to spend several hours studying each night and be excited about taking tricky tests, but we can challenge them with well-designed, differentiated, and useful assessments so they can learn and experience successes from meeting challenges. That will excite them.

How to Give Formative Assessments to Help Students Accept Critical Feedback

Helping students accept and want critical feedback is essential to getting them ready for college and their careers. Like most things, exposing students to the skills we want them to learn and then giving them many opportunities to practice are the most effective ways of building these skills. It's kind of like bowling. There are some unusual things about bowling you can directly apply to improving classroom learning, so let's go bowling for a minute. Imagine you are at a bowling alley. You brought your own beautiful bowling ball, and you are wearing your stylishly patterned bowling shoes. As soon as you step up to the lane, however, someone ties a blindfold over your eyes so you can't see a thing. Undaunted, you launch your ball down the lane, and you hear the solid crash of a ball against pins. But there is so much noise in the building that you can't tell whether it was your ball or someone else's. You wonder, "Did I get a strike, or was it a gutter ball?"

How long do you think you would continue to bowl if you could not see what you were aiming at, and you never knew if you even hit a pin? I know I wouldn't last very long. It would be pointless. The most enjoyable thing about bowling is seeing how you did after each throw. You are in charge of your own performance, and you get to see the results as a natural consequence. As with any endeavor, if you do it enough, you can often get pretty good at it, which is even more fun. Bowling is one of many learning systems that give participants intrinsic feedback to improve, and feedback is the most important element of formative assessment.

Education, like bowling, is most fun and effective when the learner is in charge of his own improvement. He sees the goal, gives his best shot at meeting it, gets feedback to make corrections, and then tries again. If the bowler does not knock down all ten pins on the first roll, he gets another chance to knock down the ones still standing. The bowler is dependent on being able to see what happens when the ball he has just released strikes the pins. The next time he rolls the ball, he applies what he learned from the first roll to do it better. If it works, great! He's achieved success. If it doesn't, then it is not failure. He simply tries again. Everyone is a lousy bowler the first go-round. It's the repetition that makes us better. So why do we expect our students to knock down all ten content pins the first time they pick up the ball?

S T R A T E G Y

Peer Review

This strategy does not just mean having students exchange papers to grade. In order for it to work, you first must trust students be serious on how they grade. Most students would much rather be graded by the teacher, but that is not the point of this exercise. The point of the exercise is that the grader will have to critique a peer's paper and provide suggestions on how to improve it. Just as a teacher learns much more about a subject in the preparation for teaching than do the students, the peer evaluator will learn a tremendous amount by evaluating another student's work. Additionally, the concepts on the checklist and the rubric are reinforced as students have to read them and evaluate a peer. The other thing that the teacher must do is provide a bit of training on how this should be done. A simple framework form, like the one that follows in Figure 7.1, will help students focus on providing effective critiques.

TECHNIQUE: Peer review rubric. The other thing that the teacher can make available to help students provide effective peer review is a detailed rubric of the assignment (see Figure 7.2). If the rubric is given to all the students before they begin working on the assignment, there are no surprises when the same form is used to critique their performance. This form makes it easy for students to objectively consider if all of the elements of the assignment have been completed. It also make grading very easy; for example, one point for the first column, two points for the second, and three for the fourth. Students simply count how many checkmarks in each column and, for the second and third columns multiply by two and three, respectively, then add the totals from all three columns.

TECHNIQUE: Peer review process paper: Hamburger format. As described earlier in this chapter, critiques are more palatable when they are sandwiched between two compliments. Have the students practice in their peer review sessions, writing or saying one compliment, a suggestion for improvement, and another compliment as they provide feedback on rough drafts.

Figure 7.1 TECHNIQUE: Peer review checklist

Writing Guides	1–5	Notes for Peer Review
Genre		
Style		
Tone		
Mechanics		
Spelling		
Grammar		
Punctuation		
Organization		
Thesis statement		
Introductory paragraph		
Body		
Conclusion		
Detail		
Facts		
Opinions		
Evidence		
Examples		
Authority		
Sources		
References		
Validity		

S T R A T E G Y

Rough Draft

The key to effective formative assessment is clear and direct feedback. This feedback can be given orally with a few short phrases, "Please review your initial statement and see if what you just wrote supports that." Or "When you correctly labeled the part of the cell, what was the most difficult part about telling the organelles apart?" It can be given in a written note on paper, "I particularly enjoyed the section where you talked about fooling the dog to chase someone else instead of you." It can be a rubric as we have discussed above, or it can be thoughtful comments, suggestions, and hints placed on a rough draft. The rough draft is a powerful formative assessment and tool that can be used in any content area. Below are three applications of providing rough draft learning experiences.

Figure 7.2 TECHNIQUE: Peer review rubric

Needs Work	Nearly There	Adequate
Genre		
Writing style may be evident. Too much or too little description.	Writing style is inconsistent. Ideas may be disjointed. Description too detailed.	Writing style makes it easy to read and to follow the ideas. Not too descriptive.
Too much tone or not enough tone.	The tone is over the top in some instances.	The tone is appropriate for the genre. Not overbearing or caustic. Generally happy.
Mechanics		
Several spelling errors.	Few spelling errors.	No spelling errors.
Several grammatical errors.	Few grammatical errors.	No grammatical errors.
Punctuation is an obstacle to understanding or is missing.	Punctuation causes confusion in some cases.	Punctuation aids comprehension and ease of reading.
Organization		
Thesis statement is missing or not identifiable.	Thesis is identifiable, but not clear.	Clearly stated thesis.
Introductory paragraph is missing or incomplete.	Introduces the main ideas, but not creatively.	Introduction is interesting and engaging.
Some of the body supports the thesis statement.	Most of the body supports the thesis statement.	Body supports the thesis statement.
Conclusion reviews some of the thesis statement or is incomplete.	Most of the thesis statement is reviewed in the conclusion.	The thesis points are reviewed in the conclusion.
Detail		
Some of the facts are faulty or incorrect.	Few of the facts appear faulty.	Data appear to be factual.
Some opinion is given the same status as fact.	Most opinion is treated with caution.	Opinion is treated with caution.
Some statements are supported by evidence, examples.	Most statements supported by evidence, examples.	Statements are supported by evidence, examples.
Authority		
Some references are listed and cited.	Most references are listed and cited.	References are listed and cited.
Some sources for references are valid and reliable.	Most sources for references are valid and reliable.	The sources for the references are valid and reliable.

TECHNIQUE: *Math process rough draft.* Too often we consider mathematics all numbers and abstract concepts when in fact it is a rich language full of communication. Math has its own set of vocabulary and phraseology and its own methods of expression. In fact, the numbers and symbols we all learn to adore in math are actually a shorthand for the real communication that being shared. $X + 5 = 25$ is really saying that in to get 25 things, you must add a certain number of things to the five things you already have. In manipulation of the sentence to read $X = 25 - 5$, I can rephrase it to say if I subtract the five things I have from the total that I want, that leaves the number I have yet to acquire as 20 things. When students can not only describe in words what an equation is really saying but also the process for arriving at a solution then they are actually conversant in the language of math.

A math teacher can ask the students to write two paragraphs about a math problem. The first paragraph will explain what the math problem is communicating, i.e., what it means. The second paragraph will describe what methods the student might use to solve the problem. The students submit this as the rough draft and the teacher provides feedback for each student. This process can also be accomplished in a peer review format.

TECHNIQUE: *Science experiment rough draft.* The general rule for science experiments in schools is that they are performed once (summative). Students must get all the data and draw the conclusions from that singular dataset. In reality, no industrial or academic scientist would only perform an experiment one time and expect to get valid data. When I was in high school, I remember feeling very frustrated that my antacid tablets did not absorb the expected amount of acid. I am sure that had I been given at least two other opportunities to perform the experiment that the numbers would have averaged closer to the ideal. Just doing the experiment again would not have aided accuracy or deepened learning unless I had performed a personal evaluation of the experiment and reflected on why the data was so off-kilter. In this way, I could determine what to adjust on the next go-round. This reflection should be done in the lab notebooks between each iteration of the experiment. (Due to money and time constraints it is understandable that there is pressure to only do a particular experiment once. In those situations, consider combining experiments from several students to get more accurate data. Students would still perform the reflection in their lab manuals but afterwards would share their reflections with the other members of their trio or team.)

TECHNIQUE: *History lessons learned rough draft.* It is said that those who do not study history are doomed to repeat it. I would add that those who attempt to study history without repetition and feedback will never learn the lessons of history. Whether it is recent company history or ancient Roman history, students must be able to look at the original historical documents and piece together a story of what actually happened. Then students can draw conclusions from historical facts to create a lessons learned draft.

1. The first draft is an outline flowchart or graphical organizer: this action started everything, which led to that action, and then to another action, etc. This first draft is peer reviewed to provide feedback on the logical connections and flow.
2. The next draft is still a flowchart but the outlined bullets for each action are now converted to sentences with one addition. Between each action there is a connecting sentence: This relates to that because ... or ..., because of that, this became necessary, etc. This draft is also peer reviewed with a focus on the connections.
3. In the next draft, students will put it all together in paragraph form to be reviewed by the teacher who will make comments and suggestions for the final draft.

S T R A T E G Y

Validation

When performing research, the first steps to take are to establish the hypothesis and then create a series of questions that you would need answered in order to support your hypothesis. Sometimes you take a survey or a questionnaire as part of the research. Any tool that is used as part of the research should be validated first. Validating research tools means that other eyes need to review the tool and provide feedback as to its effectiveness and its accuracy. This could be simply having expert colleagues look it over or sending it off to well-known experts to review. The whole point of validation is to get feedback for improving.

TECHNIQUE: *Gallery walk.* Each group of four or five students creates a poster representing the best symbolism of the literature. For example, eighth graders would be able to identify the problems (plots) and the effectiveness of the solutions in the story *The War of the Worlds* by H. G. Wells. For example: "Confronted with the reality that man is insignificant compared to more advanced beings," "Fear of being caught and the motivation of survival," "Human desire to fight back against impossible odds," "Witness the metamorphosis of humanity when placed in dire circumstances," "Revelation of what is most important in this life," "Struggling with despair." Once the posters are displayed on the walls, each group stands up and travels about the room, critiquing each poster. On sticky notes, each group writes a question or makes a comment. After all the posters have been reviewed, each group looks at the comments and writes a reflection about what they learned by reviewing other posters, and what they learned by reading the comments and questions of the other groups. Then the posters (or other work) come down and each author then makes revisions based on the feedback received.

TECHNIQUE: Solute versus solution. A solution is like water and sugar. Once they are mixed, they are not easily separated. They become a single unit. The solute is what is being dissolved, the sugar; the solvent is what does the dissolving, the water. Students' task is to identify the elements of the literature that are so intertwined as to be viewed as a single element, when in fact they are multiple elements. Shakespeare was a master at weaving different parts of his plays with different elements that seem to flow together. Perhaps the best example of this is *A Midsummer Night's Dream*, in which reality and surrealism exist seamlessly in the same space. In the same way, we want students to integrate corrections and improvements to make it a seamless piece.

Once the teacher has returned a paper with comments and suggestions, the student will then try to integrate those suggestions and comments into the next revision. To aid the student in doing this, the student will write solute as a head on one column and solution as the head on another. The comments and suggestions from the reviewer go in the solute column. The student then looks at each comment in the left-hand column and describes what he needs to do to integrate that comment into his work and writes that in the solution column.

TECHNIQUE: Butterfly learning. As a butterfly will flit from one flower to another gathering sweet nectar, students can do the same thing. Students post a piece of work on the wall to be commented on by their peers. Often, this means that the only comments that a student actually sees are the ones he made or the ones others made on his paper. To allow a larger picture, once all the comments are on the students' papers, then students will take another tour of the room and look closely at the comments. Direct the students to find three things from others' comments that resonate with them. Have them incorporate them into their own papers in the next revision.

Notes

1 Clint Eastwood's 1966 film, *The Good, the Bad and the Ugly*, has a special place in my heart. My wife and I had just returned from our honeymoon and were settling in our new place. We decided that we wanted to watch the video of our wedding reception. We pulled out the video cassette that a friend had videotaped for us and sat down to enjoy. Lo and behold, instead, we saw a recording of Clint Eastwood's *The Good, the Bad, and the Ugly*. Little did we know then what we were in for (is that foreshadowing?). Anyway, we are still together and all our children are on their own, and amidst all the struggles and heartaches, we still love each other. We did find the real tape eventually. Luckily it had not been recorded over, but it gave us a scare, and a laugh.

2 Cisco Inc. has a marvelous program, the Cisco Networking Academy, which schools can take advantage of to help students become certified Cisco Networking Technicians. In order to establish a training facility on your campus, a teacher must attend the training first and become certified. Then for a minimum amount of money, the school can purchase the necessary laboratory equipment (routers, switches, and hubs) on which students can practice. Students who attend such a lab will be able to complete their initial networking certification before going to a trade school or college. For more information, go to https://www.netacad.com/.

Willingness to Adjust Based on Feedback

Willing to Adjust Learning: Capacity to Alter Course Mid-stream

Why Do Students Need to Be Willing to Adjust Their Learning?

As we learned earlier, when you bowl, you get to see where the ball goes and what the result is, strike or spare. In basketball, you see the ball's arc and hear the swish or else you have to go for the rebound. In softball, while swinging the bat you hear the crack and see the ball zooming away or you hear the smack of the catcher's mitt. Each of these is an example of immediate feedback that informs the athletes and allows them to improve on the next turn. The same could be said of any sport that requires aim. Having the opportunity to shoot more than once serves to improve the score by using what was learned from previous shots. But interestingly enough, being able to try again and strive for this very improvement is the sole exhilaration and motivation for participating in the sport in the first place. How interesting would bowling be if the bowling ball were only rolled down the alley once? What would be the draw of baseball if the pitcher were only allowed one pitch for each batter? There are some obvious connections to education here. Far too often in education, we do not provide immediate feedback to students, and by this failure to do so, in a single stroke, we eliminate the sole exhilaration and motivation for learning in the first place.

Flexibility Is Fomented by Feedback—
True Formative Assessment

Not only does my example show immediate feedback, but it is also shows Formative Assessment. (How is that for awesome alliteration? FFF.) By "formative" I mean "having the capacity to form, or being capable of altering the form of something malleable." That sounds amazingly similar to what we perceive that educators do in general. We change a student from being stupid to smart, unintelligent to intelligent, uninformed to informed, unskillful to skillful, ignorant to knowledgeable, and so on. If we follow this reasoning, then as teachers we are doing all the work and should get all the credit, right? Hang on there. Doesn't this sound awfully boastful of us? Are we really doing all that? Are students simple lumps of clay to be molded to the form deemed most appropriate by the teachers? Are they glowing pieces of iron that teachers hammer into useful tools? To tell you the truth, I think that we would be presuming too much if we even hinted that teachers are the ones who make changes like those happen. Students, not teachers, are the ones who are the protagonists in the learning process.

The *tabula rasa* metaphor doesn't seem to explain what really happens in teaching and learning. We need to find another metaphor that more closely matches what education is really about. I think I have found one. Here it goes. Let's change the teacher's hammer for a whistle and the lump of clay for an athlete. Yes, that's better. Not new, you say? Well of course there are other metaphors, symphony conductor and musicians for example, but since we started this conversation with a sports theme, let's stick with the sports theme. Now in terms of a sports team being led by the coach, what is the role of the athlete? It is to learn and apply what is learned. The coach provides immediate feedback by giving the athletes either individual information concerning performance or general information for the team. Once this given, the coach says, "Try it again." During each iteration of the skill (or time at bat), the coach gives immediate feedback, but it is the athletes who are willingly sweating, struggling, and expending all that energy. Each time the skill is performed, the athletes improve—they turn themselves into better athletes. Through practice and listening to good coaching (teaching), students increase their stamina, strength, and skill. Most successful coaches do not have to coerce their team members to perform because when athletes see improvement, that is motivation enough to push them to keep on sweating, struggling, and expending all that energy. At times, the coach needs to point out the progress or lack of progress (assessment). If the latter, this is immediately followed by, "Do it over again." Believe it or not, we are now back to where we started. Who is it that is doing the "forming" in formative assessments? It is obvious that it is the athletes. So why do we find it so difficult to use this model in our classrooms?

"We do use this model!" you say.

Respectfully, I ask the following questions. "Students willingly sweat, struggle, and expend all sorts of energy in your classes? You give pretests and posttests so students can judge their performance and measure the improvement? You provide rubrics of expected performance before students are expected to perform? You provide constant immediate feedback regarding students' academic progress? If students don't do well, you let them do it again?"

You may answer that you do some of these things regularly, but if we use the coach and athlete metaphor as a comparison, I believe that all of you would agree that the education that occurs in most classrooms is not nearly as "active" as what happens out on the athletic fields. One of the glaring missing elements in the typical classroom learning cycle is the "formative assessment" process that happens naturally on the athletic field. True formative assessment engages students and puts them in charge of their own learning, much as a bowler is in charge of how he or she bowls.

> The only way that an assessment can be formative is if the student can learn from the assessment. Students only learn from the assessment if they have a chance to take it again.

Although information gained from tests and quizzes helps teachers know what, when, and how well to teach, formative assessment should not be solely for the teacher. It should primarily be for the student. The student is the one "forming" himself or herself. The opposite of formative is summative, or "game over" assessment. The critical role of the teacher in formative assessment is to provide the student with feedback and the opportunity to improve by repeating the task.[1] In order for an assessment to be "formative," students must be able to do the three things shown in Figure 8.1.

How to Help Students Adjust Based on Feedback

How can students know how to react and adjust to feedback if they receive precious little of it? Our job as educators is to give them as much immediate

Figure 8.1 Formative Assessment Cycle

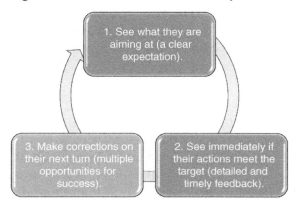

feedback as we can. This is more than saying "Good job!" or giving a pat on the back. General verbal feedback has its place, and is essential to a good classroom climate, but the feedback that helps students learn from mistakes is the specific, targeted feedback that illuminates the problem and gives suggestions on how to fix it. For example, a coach might say, "Joe, you're not making the shots because you don't give the ball enough arc. Try it this way and see if it helps." A math teacher might say, "Jessie, you are having trouble with fractions because you might be confusing the numerator with the denominator. Think of it this way: A denominator is like the word denominations. It means types of money. If I give you two of these (you pull out two one-dollar bills and a five-dollar bill), how many one-dollar bills do I have? If this were a fraction, you would write two over five. So the denominator is a type of number that indicates how many pieces a whole is divided into, like five one-dollar bills go into a five-dollar bill. The numerator sits on top and tells how many of the denominators there are. A dollar is how many fifths of a five-dollar bill? So, 2/3 is how many thirds?"

The other feedback that students desperately need comes from formative assessments aligned to the learning standards. Grant Wiggins and Jay McTighe (1998) wrote *Understanding by Design* and explained how teachers need to start with the formative assessment and build learning activities that directly prepare students to be successful. Remember that in order for assessment to be "formative," students have to receive the timely feedback that is specific enough to identify the problem and how to fix it, and then they need to have an opportunity to do it again. A quiz is not formative unless students get the results back promptly and have a chance to take the quiz (the same one or a version of it) again, and if the quiz is aligned then teachers can track student progress by objective.[2]

What Kinds of Formative Assessment Can a Teacher Create to Provide Immediate Feedback to Students?

Perhaps the most recognizable formative assessment is having students do a rough draft, which we have already mentioned. In the rough draft process, students submit their first draft for review, get feedback on their writing, and then make corrections and submit their work again. Though this is time-consuming, especially on the first drafts, if the teacher provides effective feedback, later drafts will be much improved and eventually will end up saving time because the students learned (i.e., they know how to do it) and do not need to be reminded in future assignments.

We have already discussed the topic of using questions to prompt students to think analytically, critically, and creatively. As a reminder, asking a verbal question in class and hoping some student will answer it is not the best way to ask questions. For starters, it is not a formative assessment, because it does not provide individual feedback to each student, nor do students have an opportunity to repeat their performance. The other problem with the typical "class discussion model" is that only one student is engaged at a time. Nevertheless, there are ways to make verbal questioning an excellent formative-assessment method and engage all students. This simple method is to ask all the students to answer the same question at the same time, and then provide individual feedback. (Remember Total Physical Response [TPR] discussed in chapter 2?)

For example, you could have students give a thumbs-up or thumbs-down gesture in response to a statement you make. They can all touch the correct word on a displayed visual. They can put their finger on the evidence that supports their answer in the book. They can stand up if they think the answer you've given is correct or sit on the floor if they have an answer different from the one you gave. They can stand in one corner if the answer is A, or in another corner if it's B. They can lift their right hand for true or left for false. There are many other creative ways to have students all show they understand. TPR is quick, easy, and provides good feedback to the students and teacher. A side product of these techniques is that students also get feedback from looking at what other students are doing, and if they are out of sync with the rest of the class, they usually correct their choices without a teacher having to intervene. Then the correct answer from the teacher simply reinforces what they've already learned just moments before. Teachers can tell right away how many students understand and how many don't when they ask students to demonstrate what they know in this way. Then the teacher can immediately adjust instruction to make sure every student understands before going on to the next learning objective. A similar method makes use of individual electronic keypads, computer programs, "clickers," student polling devices, or even small personal whiteboards, similar to the slates each student had in classrooms long ago. Students write their answers and hold them up so the teacher and all the other students can see.

To help students become flexible and resilient in receiving feedback, they must receive constant sources of feedback. In order for your assessments to be truly formative, you have to set clear standards and expectations of performance, provide detailed and timely feedback, and then give students multiple opportunities to learn from their mistakes to achieve mastery. As teachers, we must provide frequent formative assessments to students so they can see well enough to quit bowling gutter balls and start throwing strikes. Following are some strategies and associated techniques that will help you do this.

S T R A T E G Y

Rough Drafts

Learning takes time and energy on the part of the learner and the teacher. One of the most time-intensive yet rewarding strategies available is commonly known as the rough draft. The English language arts folks are well acquainted with this strategy; however, as mentioned earlier, rough drafts can be used in any content area. The concept is basically thus: students submit a paper fleshed out with ideas and written in readable narrative form. The teacher reads through the paper, bleeds all over it (corrects it with a red pen), makes suggestions for improvement, and returns it to the student. With this new information about the content, students can now rewrite the paper, fixing the mistakes. The paper is then resubmitted and corrected cyclically until it is error-free. This may take several iterations, or if the student is a quick study, only one iteration.

TECHNIQUE: Movie critic. Movie critics have to come up with a snazzy line that says what they feel about a movie. When peer reviewing another's work, students come up with their own one-liners about their general impression of the work, taglines for the more in-depth analysis to follow. This forces students to acknowledge the primary strengths and weaknesses in creative, higher-order thinking ways.

"Bring your pillow for this essay full of trite, uninspired ideas!"
"You might need your seatbelt for this rollercoaster of a narrative!"
"The cast of *Law and Order* could not improve on this argument!"

TECHNIQUE: Critique assembly line. One of the things that the assembly line did for the production of automobiles was to create automobiles in a hurry. Each assembly line worker became an expert at the one task he or she was assigned. Assign peer review topics to different teams of students. Each team only reviews for their topic, then passes the papers on to the next team. One benefit of this method is that the reviews will probably be more objective because of so many raters. Before the peer review begins, you may want to perform some inter-rater reliability to make sure all the members of the team evaluate the same paper the same. For example, you assign one team of students to check for grammar mistakes, another team to look for supporting evidence, and a third team to evaluate the support of the thesis statements and the conclusion.

TECHNIQUE: Partner review. Have students use the peer review checklist to review a partner's paper. Once completed, the partner will review the other partner's paper. Then the papers are submitted with the reviews, which are also part of the grade.

S T R A T E G Y

Test Retake Policy

The concept behind this strategy is that students must fix the errors they committed on a test, assessment, or evaluation, include explanations (not excuses) of why they got certain parts wrong, and finally, show they have learned by retaking the test, assessment, or evaluation with questions similar to the ones they missed the first time. Formative assessments based on learning objectives are powerful tools for tracking student progress, class progress, and teacher effectiveness on specific learning objectives. What I mean by this is that every question of a quiz is identified with a particular learning objective that was taught in the class. As the instruction proceeds and these aligned assessments are taken, teachers can track student progress (mastery) by objective, which is much more powerful than simply giving students an A, B, or C, or percentage grades on the assessment as a whole.

While a plethora of data analysis tools exist for disaggregating student performance by objective, it takes the persistence of a dedicated teacher to utilize them consistently. If done correctly, a teacher can know—with more certainty than any district benchmark could provide—how well each of his or her students would perform on the state standardized test.

TECHNIQUE: *Same exact test.* A convenient method to make student assessment a learning process is to allow students to take the same exact test again to improve the score. However, it is not fair to students who did well on the test and will not be taking the test again if a retaker gets the same points. Therefore, the teacher should set a sliding scale subtracting for the extra study days, or a diminishing percentage depending on the number of times the test can be taken. For example, the first time a test is given, it is worth 100 points. The second time it is worth 80 points. The third time it is worth 70 points. The fourth time it is worth 60 points. You can adjust the scale to suit your purposes. Remember this is for formative assessment and not for summative assessment. We want students to be able to perform well on the formative assessment in preparation for the summative assessment.

TECHNIQUE: *Objective-related test.* Especially nowadays, teachers have at their disposal item banks of questions that are aligned to certain learning objectives. The only difference from the previous technique is that the test would be a different test, but testing over the same exact objectives. This still allows the results to be disaggregated and compared to the other tests as long as they are all aligned to the same standards. To be fair to students who did not make mistakes, the grading of the corrections should not give students the opportunity for a perfect score, but should allow students to improve their grade to a certain extent.

TECHNIQUE: *Targeted test.* Your time is valuable and so is the students' time. So after a formative test has been given and you have provided specific feedback on how students can improve, here is a way you and the students desiring to take the test again can save time and energy. Especially for longer tests, and considering multiple retakes for formative tests, a great way to save time and focus on what improvement is really needed is to have the student retake only the parts of the test they get wrong. It seems like a simple technique, but it is effective.

S T R A T E G Y

Personal Conversations

One of the largest issues in developing academic relationships through personal conversations with every student is time. Another big issue is classroom management. We find time to pull failing or struggling students aside to discuss their progress and how to improve it, but reaching out to each student on their progress is a daunting task because of the pressures of testing. Below are some techniques that will help manage the students and give back some time.

TECHNIQUE: Pre-parent conference. The parent has a great deal of influence over the behavior of the student, but as the student gets older, that influence wanes. Eventually, we want (and the parent wants) that student to be totally responsible for his or her own learning. In an effort to promote this, we can discuss with each student what will be discussed in the parent conference. As Susan M. Brookhart (2008) suggests in her book, *How to Give Effective Feedback to Your Students*, you need to find a place in your classroom where you can still keep an eye on what the other students are doing but at the same time have a bit of privacy. On that note, it is important to give the other students something to do that does not require your direction and that will keep them busy long enough to cover a few pre-parent–teacher conferences. Also in preparation for the pre-parent–teacher conference, you should print out a detailed grade report for each student. Plan to use the hamburger approach with each student; sandwich the one most important goal for improvement between two sincere compliments. It is not necessary to try to get all of the pre-parent–teacher conferences done in one day; it may take a week, 20 minutes at a time.

TECHNIQUE: Group oral feedback. You will find when grading papers that student work often has similar characteristics and presents similar misconceptions or errors. Another technique borrowed from Ms. Brookhart (p. 53) is to gather those students according to similarities of their work and have four or five included in one conversation. Explain why they are all there, be sure to compliment them on their similar strengths, and then discuss with them your thoughts on how they can all improve. This technique, due to the critical mass of students, has the added benefit of being easier to engage in discussions and brainstorm possible solutions than if you were talking to one student only.

TECHNIQUE: High performance learning team pep talks. Students, like anyone, love to be a part of a winning team. Students often need refocusing and encouragement from the teacher and their peers. Take a few minutes every month; it could be the sponge activity for that day, to pass out sticky notes to each student. Instruct the student to select the person on their left, or in front of them or their partner (or any way that makes sure that each student gets a note from someone; odd-numbered students get a note from the teacher). You can be creative with who the notes go to. If you write an encouraging note or compliment and a "keep up the good work" message monthly, the students will know what to do.

Notes

1 Grant Wiggins, one of the foremost authorities on assessment, wrote an excellent article for Edutopia explaining the need for more formative assessment. Read what he says about "feedback" at www.edutopia.org/authentic-assessment-grant-wiggins.
2 If each question on the quiz correlates to a specific learning objective (one that is also used for the state test), then the data gathered from the quiz will show how your students performed on each objective and over time will show progress toward mastery the more aligned quizzes you give them. This is what is meant by alignment, and it is a power-ful concept aided greatly by advances in the technological ability to gather and disaggre-gate the results by objective. For more information on this topic, see Douglas Reeves' book on assessment. It is an anthology of the thoughts of the best and the brightest leaders on how to use assessment to improve teaching and learning: Reeves, D. (2007), *Ahead of the Curve: The Power of Assessment to Transform Teaching and Learning*. Bloomington, IN: Solution Tree Press.

References

Brookhart, S. M. (2008). *How to Give Effective Feedback to Your Students*. Alex-andria, VA: Association for Supervision and Curriculum Development.

Reeves, D. (2007), *Ahead of the Curve: The Power of Assessment to Transform Teaching and Learning*. Bloomington, IN: Solution Tree Press.

Wiggins, G. and McTighe, J. (1998). *Understanding by Design*. Alexandria, VA: Association for Supervision and Curriculum Development.

Chapter 9

Openness to Possible Failure

Openness to Failure: Willingness to Trust and Take Academic Risks

Why Do Students Need to Be Open to Possible Failure?

I was the assistant superintendent of a small school district located just thirty miles south of San Antonio, Texas, with a total school population of 1,100 students. Even though people consider it a rural district, its existence is anything but bucolic. Natalia is a bedroom community for San Antonio, and as such, IN to deal with many big-city issues. The population is 75 percent Hispanic, but only about 15 percent of those Hispanic students actually speak Spanish, and a very small percentage of those learned English as a second language. The district's biggest concerns were the achievement gaps that existed between white and Hispanic students and the overall mentality of underachievement. Although I wore many hats in my position, the one that felt most comfortable was the one relating to curriculum and instruction—in particular, helping teachers maximize their instructional power and overcome barriers to student learning.

If you haven't noticed by now, I am a pragmatist, and I believe in simple, systemic solutions. I firmly believe that the true art/skill/magic/science of teaching is to perfectly match your style with the individual student's needs. Conceptually, many teachers know this is the right way to teach. However, it flies in the face of what most teaching professionals practice. Today, more often than not, it is the students who must adapt or fail. Teaching in the truest sense of the word comes down to what you believe about students and what you believe is the best way to teach them. This is what I believe. As an example of this, I would like to share a short story. A shaggy but beautiful stray dog came to our house one day. Our hearts went out to it, and we decided to help it. We put out some food, which it ate, but it refused to let us approach. Every time we tried, it would shy away and stay out of reach. As much as we wanted to be of more help to the dog, it would not let us. The bottom line is that for one reason or another, it did not trust us. Who knows what its history was? It trusted us enough to eat our food, but that was as far as it went. I am sure that, given a few weeks, we could have built a relationship of trust with that dog—but unfortunately it moved on and we haven't seen it since.

Students who come to our classrooms are much like that dog (with cell phones to distract them instead of fleas). Unless the students trust us, they are unapproachable. Imagine being asked to ride a two-seater bicycle across a tightrope with somebody you do not trust steering the bicycle. We earn our students' trust by showing them respect in the form of meaningful, challenging, and rewarding learning activities that are worthy of their time and best efforts. This kind of trust has to be developed early in the student's tightrope riding (education) career, otherwise no student in their right mind would attempt it. Students in their early years of school are naturally trusting, and—please don't take this the wrong way—we often abuse that trust in the name of socialization and classroom management. In order to control large numbers of students at the same time, we teach them to obey rather than to explore. Because of this, as students get older, they often trust less and start behaving much like our shaggy and suspicious visitor. Most will take what we offer but will not allow a lasting learning partnership to develop. Trust works the other way, too. As teachers, we have learned to distrust our students. All it takes is one disruptive young person to ruin it for the rest of the students who follow. We don't want to get burned again, so we tighten the rules and narrow the focus. We develop an attitude that we can't trust our students to learn independently. Especially in the early grades, we feel it is our responsibility to control every aspect of the learning activities so things

> Students and teachers working together can achieve substantial learning gains.
>
> Teachers working by themselves will achieve nothing.

don't get out of hand, or so they don't make a mess, or so things do not get too loud. We could call this way of thinking the color-between-the-lines syndrome: We like everything neat and orderly.

So by the time students get to high school, some know how to color between the lines and are successful in school, while others do poorly or drop out because they are not even interested in coloring and will purposefully color outside the lines to make their point. Many times, like our beautiful stray dog, students have taken a risk and have been burned, which teaches them never to take a risk again. This is especially evident in math. I had a math teacher who scared me to death. He demanded that we learn the properties and theorems of algebra and be able to recite them word-for-word when he called our student number (not even our name). I was always petrified that he would call on me. To this day, I cringe when I hear the algebraic postulates. Luckily, I had teachers after that who related better to students and math, so much so that I minored in math in college. Anyway, I know that my algebra teacher meant well—knowing the rules of algebra is essential to being successful in algebra—but the method he used was unsuccessful for me, and I would assume for many of his students. All too often, students never recover from math or science shock and, as a result, go out of their way to avoid anything related to math or science.

Teachers inhibit risk-taking in other ways without even recognizing that that is what they are doing. For example, by always insisting that students shut up and listen to you, you send the clarion message, "What I have to say is more important than anything you might say." There is no way students can compete with that, and if they try, many times we view their questions as challenges, as being insubordinate and disrespectful. The idea that teachers have all the answers is ludicrous. Equally ludicrous is the prevalent idea that students have none of the answers. I once had a student teacher who taught the introduction to psychology courses at a high school. I gave her an assignment to prepare a pretest and a posttest for one of her psychology lessons. She protested the pretest because, in her words, "My students don't know anything about psychology; it is therefore pointless to test them prior to instruction!"

I couldn't believe the arrogance emanating from this teacher. There is a solution to this: student-centered learning, or, better stated, student-directed learning. I say student-directed learning because it is too easy to mistake the idea of focusing all of the teacher's attention on students as student-centeredness. If you as the teacher are making all of the decisions about what to study and how to study it, then it is really teacher-centered learning. As discussed earlier with formative assessments, the student is the one doing the heavy lifting of learning. In order to motivate students and help them be willing to do the sweating, struggling, and energy expending required of learning, we must allow a certain amount of student independence and choice. Teaching is just as much about taking risks as learning is. A teacher has to take a chance on students and trust them enough to be independent learners. That can't happen if the teacher is uncomfortable about tailoring the curriculum to multiple levels of student performance.[1]

A Teaching Personal Philosophy Is Crucial

As I stated earlier, teaching styles flow from what an educator believes is the "best way to teach students." That belief is not demonstrated in mission statements and platitudes, but it is clearly visible in the way teachers set up and run their classrooms and in how they treat their students. This is the personal teaching philosophy. Once a teacher truly understands the mechanics of the learning cycle, discipline and classroom management take a secondary role, and the teacher can focus on what he or she can do to help all of his or her students learn best, whatever it takes. Basic to student-directed learning is that we have to trust students enough to give them formative learning opportunities we sometimes call assessments. We have to trust students to master content sufficiently in order to collaborate with their peers on project-based learning, investigations, explorations, and inquiry. We have to trust that students, given the right learning environment, will learn. We have to show trust in our students as the protagonists of the learning process by providing them opportunities to show what they have learned rather than always depending on paper and pencil assessment. Above all, we need to develop that trust in the early grades. Otherwise, we will end up trying unsuccessfully to teach a bunch of skittish stray dogs for students.

How to Help Students Be Open to Possible Failure

As discussed earlier, trust is the basic element of any relationship, but it is even more so for teaching and learning. When students trust their teachers, they can be more frank with their vulnerabilities. And such lucky teachers, because of that trust, can push these students to higher standards than would ordinarily be possible. One of the college- and career-readiness skills that university professors who participated in the University of Oregon study on college readiness wish their students had is the ability to face the fact that they will not succeed at everything. Sometimes students will fail (English, 2000).[2] Students will face multitudes of obstacles they will have to overcome in order to be successful; they cannot afford to wimp out at the first sign of trouble. Unfortunately, too many students do not recover from failure, as demonstrated in the 2003 statistics from the ACT report called *Reading between the Lines: What the ACT Reveals about College Readiness in Reading*. More than 3,000 students drop out of high school every day, primarily because they do not possess the literacy skills to keep up with the curriculum. Sometimes even students who make it to college are not able to face failures. Approximately 11 percent of students in college are enrolled in remedial reading coursework, and 75 percent of them will not obtain their degrees in eight years (ACT, 2006).

Learning involves opening up and exposing our vulnerability, trusting, taking risks, and becoming resilient about the outcomes. Taking risks involves many complex psychological and behavioral functions. One of the things that I learned as a foreign language teacher is that each person has what is called an affective filter ("affective" meaning dealing with emotions).[3] When we feel intimidated or afraid of how others will respond, or have a fear of being spotlighted, our affective filter clamps down, thinking stops, and we are left with the primal fight or flight choices. According to neuroscientists, this is a physiological response to an infusion of cortisol, a neuropeptide that inhibits logic function by blocking transmission of neural messages in the hippocampus (this is the organ that is associated strongly with learning and memory). What this means is that when we experience strong negative emotion, cortisol is released and the thinking part of the brain is inhibited, leaving us with the primal part of the brain that worries only about survival. Constant stress, or chronic stress, can lead to destruction of neurons in the hippocampus that could even cause "brain damage" (see Figure 9.1).

As we've discussed earlier, students are fairly adept at avoiding and minimizing their exposure to situations in which they are placed in the public spotlight. For this reason, they sit in the back of the room, they do not raise their hands, and they basically keep a low profile in your classroom. In previous chapters, we've also discussed the traditional teacher-questioning routine: ask a general question and let whichever student raises their hand first answer it. In general, we know who those students are. There is an easy fix for lowering the affective filter so students do not need to hide in your classroom.

The most effective way to reduce the affective filter is to reduce the size of the audience. For students, it is much easier to make mistakes in front of one or two students than to be exposed to the ridicule of the whole class witnessing inadequacies and failures. As teachers, we must be sensitive to the climate of the class and the levels of stress that it maintains.

This does not mean that all stress is bad. There is another type of stress called eustress that is good stress and makes our bodies respond in a positive manner. Eustress is experienced by students when they are given challenging

Figure 9.1 The Effects of Stress on the Brain

circumstances but they feel prepared to face them with confidence. In this case, another neuropeptide is released called endorphins. Athletes feel the effects of endorphins during workouts. This is sometimes known as the "runner's high," not surprisingly because this peptide mimics the effects of opiates to reduce pain and increase a sense of euphoria.[4] We need to make sure our learning environment and learning activities minimize "stress," or challenges for which students are unprepared, and instead prepare students to be successful in rigorous learning challenges so that eustress can reduce anxiety and make them stronger (Caine and Caine, 1991). The key to developing college- and career-ready students is to cultivate in the students a state of relaxed alertness.

S T R A T E G Y

Tell Students That It Will Be Hard, but They Can Do It

Yes, it is as simple as that. I read a study that had two groups of students of similar mixes of abilities, backgrounds, and socioeconomic status. One group was told that they were going to be given very hard tasks and that they would be able to do them. The other group was told nothing. Both groups were given the same instruction and the same tasks. Guess which group did best? Simply priming the pump for success builds success.

TECHNIQUE: *Build success*. Celebrate even small successes in student learning. I'm not saying throw a party, but at least make it a big deal for the student. There are a number of reasons to do this. First, it tells the student that you noticed and that you care. Second, it adjusts the baseline measurement and the next bit of progress will be measured according to this new standard. Finally, it allows you to establish that the student can do things successfully, even when things get difficult. When they start complaining that they can't do it, you gently remind them that you have proof that they can do it. Harry Wong in his seminal work, *How to Be an Effective Teacher: The First Days of School*, suggests that celebrations should be frequent and meaningful. Whether it is a simple smiley face with a thoughtful note, or a certificate of achievement sent home, or even a positive phone call home, a celebration establishes success and builds on it.

TECHNIQUE: *Pep talks*. As part of the "framing the lesson"[5] that the book *CHAMPS: A Proactive and Positive Approach to Classroom Management* by Sprick *et al.* suggests happens before you begin teaching, the CHAMPS system of "Framing the Lesson" with the acronym CHAMPS includes establishing before you begin teaching the acceptable behaviors and the behaviors that will not be acceptable. For example, "In this lesson you will be allowed to talk quietly in your group in order to accomplish the learning task. You will have five minutes to accomplish the task and you need to stay focused and participate fully. If you have a question you must raise your hand and wait quietly for me to attend you. You are not allowed out of your seat without permission. If your group finishes early, wait quietly for the time limit. When you have successfully completed the assignment, turn your papers over." Include a few words about the big picture of why the students need to know what you are teaching. Ask for their best work and cooperation and promise that they will be prepared to use this knowledge. Let them know that it will be difficult, but you are confident in their abilities. If there are students who disregard the frame, gently remind them of the expectations and ask them, "I know you can perform better than this. What should you be doing now?"

TECHNIQUE: *Affirmations and conclusions*. Reflections are a powerful way to help students evaluate their progress. After students have answered questions in their reflections like, "Name three specific things that I learned in this unit.

What did I enjoy the most?" Have the students create in their journals a specific affirmation, such as "You are excellent in long division! You know your pre-Columbian history like the back of your hand! You are awesome at persuasive essays!" and one conclusion, "You need to take the homework seriously. You should attend tutorials. You should leave your phone in your pocket, etc. ...."

S T R A T E G Y

Pretesting

Research has been done to determine if pretesting does any good, or perhaps a better way to put it, if failing to answer questions correctly on a pretest poses an inhibitor of future learning. The findings are conclusive. Pretesting not only provides a preview of future learning and sets up a scaffold into which the future knowledge can be placed, but it also helps students learn better. The tests that were performed had three groups of college students. One group was given extra time to study a specially prepared text with bolded key words. Another group was given a pretest, and the final group was the control group. When the results were analyzed, the pretest group outscored the group that was given extra study time with the bolded key words, even after a week of separation.[6] Pretesting has other benefits too. It makes sure that the instructor covers what the instructor says he is going to cover. Too often teachers make up the test after instruction has occurred, which leaves room for gaps in content due to instructors' bird-walking (getting off topic, or spending inordinate amounts of time on pet topics). A pretest lets the students know what is important to remember, and even though they fail the pretest, the exposure will aid long-term memory of the content as long as the teacher makes sure that it is covered. (If they pass the pretest, then the teacher should be smart enough to skip that section and go on to the next one.)

TECHNIQUE: Same test. As Grant Wiggins proposes, if teachers take the time to prepare the assessments beforehand, the teacher will automatically know what the targeted learning for the day will be. When the teacher gives students the pretest, then students will know what they are supposed to learn. If the same test that is given as a pretest is given as a posttest, then the results can be directly compared, and students and the teacher will know exactly what progress was made.

TECHNIQUE: *Forms A and B.* When you create a test, create two versions of the same test. This is more than simply switching the order of the questions, though that works in a pinch. It means keeping the same difficulty and complexity as well as the learning objectives, but changing how the questions are written. Form A can be given as a pretest, and form B given as a posttest, only if the questions on form A are correlated directly with the same learning objectives used for form B.

TECHNIQUE: *Verbal four-corners pretest.* Prepare ten multiple choice questions on the topic you will be teaching. Label each of the corners of the classroom A, B, C, D.. Instruct the students to simply stand in the corner corresponding to the answer that they think is correct. Inform the students after each question what the right answer was and tally how many students got the answer right for each question. This will inform you regarding the number of students who understand each concept and perhaps allow you to compress some topics in your lesson plans to allow time for things the students do not know.

S T R A T E G Y

Building Trust with Students

Teachers typically do not trust their students, so why should students trust their teachers? Often some teachers are like the stray dog that has been kicked one too many times by uncaring students and, as a result, shy away from trusting their students while doing everything in their power not to be abused again. Breaking the cycle of mistrust is necessary for high levels of student performance. The first step for teachers is to be trustworthy themselves, establish consistent norms applied equally, create patterns of learning that work, treat students equally and fairly, and exemplify standards of professionalism in their craft as a teacher (students know good teachers from bad ones). But trust is also a two-way street. As a teacher I have to exhibit trust on a classroom basis and on an individual basis. Below you will find some techniques that may help you establish the necessary trust for your classroom.

TECHNIQUE: Support groups. The well-known teacher training program called Capturing Kids' Hearts™ uses a number of trust building techniques that have become industry standards: stand at the door and greet your students as they walk into your class, lead students in the creation of classroom norms for each class, taking time to let students share experiences. One of the techniques with which I was impressed was designed to support students as they give a presentation. Similar to the "lifeline" made famous by the television program *So You Want to Be a Millionaire,* this technique allows students to give presentations with a student they trust supporting them and helping them out if they get stuck.

TECHNIQUE: No surprises. Daily and weekly routines that matter are extremely important for students to trust and follow the teacher, but they are not the only things. Teachers must telegraph their intentions before any learning activity is begun. Why are we doing this is a question that must be answered. Objectives written on the board for every lesson help students build a framework into which they can insert the day's learning activities. A strong syllabus, a calendar of learning activities and examinations, and clear expectations of the class provide a sense of security for most students.

TECHNIQUE: Trust and support them. One of the best ways to show trust in students is to give them a responsibility or leadership calling. Whether it is the paper monitor, white board cleaner, or the classroom general manager, students appreciate it when you show confidence in their ability to carry out a necessary activity in the classroom. It is critically important that you train the students in how you would like them to carry out their assignments and touch-base with them frequently to ensure that the assignments are being fulfilled. Additionally, just telling a student to be a leader is a recipe for failure. You have to spell it out. What does a leader do? What does a leader not do? How does a leader lead other students? How can the student leaders be inclusive rather than exclusive (i.e., get more students involved)? Any classroom assignment should begin with expectations and standards for judging completion.

Notes

1   Although differentiation is not necessarily a strategy to help teachers to prepare students to be college- and career-ready, it is a way to promote individual student success by catering instruction to their needs. Carol Anne Tomlinson, the queen of differentiation, has written

several informative books that should be part of your professional library. Here is the one you really should have: Tomlinson, C. A. (2001). *How to Differentiate Instruction in Mixed Ability Classrooms* (2nd ed.). Alexandria, VA: Association for Supervision and Curriculum Development.

2   One of the problems with our system is the bell curve because it assumes that we are satisfied with a majority of our students being mediocre and 15 percent of our students failing entirely. Fenwick English describes how we should have a skewed bell curve that targets a higher percentage of highly proficient students rather than just 15 percent at the top.

3   In 1982, Dr. Stephen Krashen was a professor at the University of Southern California when he published his foundational research, *Principles and Practice in Second Language Acquisition*, and then in 1983, *The Natural Approach: Language Acquisition in the Classroom*. He maintains that learning languages is more organic than academic and should follow the same pattern that we followed when we were infants learning our native language, which includes lots of exposure to language and oral proficiency before written proficiency.

4   Robert Sylwester is an Emeritus Professor of Education at the University of Oregon. He is coauthor of the *Information Age Education* bimonthly newsletter available at http://i-a-e. org. The information about peptides and their effect on the brain came from his early book on the brain. If you want to understand more of how the student (and our) brain works, you will want to read this book: Sylwester, R. (1995) *A Celebration of Neurons: An Educator's Guide to the Human Brain*. Alexandria, VA: Association for Supervision and Curriculum Instruction.

5   CHAMPS stands for Conversation, Help, Activity, Movement, Participation, and Success.

6   Three researchers from the University of California, Irvine and Los Angeles performed a series of five tests to determine if failing a pretest made it harder to learn. What they discovered was powerful. Not only was the opposite true, but each of the tests supported that pretesting was more effective than other proven methods to enhance knowledge retention such as providing extra study time, italicizing key words, bolding key words and the teacher emphasizing the words. Even a week later, the pretested students performed better. Attempting to answer a question on a pretest and failing at it helps students learn when the information is actually taught to them later. See Richland *et al.* (2009). "The Pretesting Effect: Do Unsuccessful Retrieval Attempts Enhance Learning?" *Journal of Experimental Psychology: Applied*, 15(3), 243–57. Retrieved from MEDLINE with full-text database.

References

ACT (2006). Reading between the Lines: What the ACT Reveals about College Readiness in Reading. Retrieved March 25th, 2017 from http://www.act. org/content/dam/act/unsecured/documents/reading_report.pdf.

Caine, R. N. and Caine, G. (1991). *Teaching and the Human Brain*. Alexandria, VA: Association for Supervision and Curriculum Development.

English, F. (2000). *Deciding What to Teach and Test* (Millennial ed.). Thousand Oaks, CA: Corwin Press, Inc.

Flippen, F. (2006). *Capturing Kids' Hearts*. College Station, TX: The Flippen Group.

Krashen, S. D. (1982). *Principles and Practice in Second Language Acquisition*. Los Angeles, CA: Pergamon Press.

Krashen, S. D. Terrell, T. D. (1995). *The Natural Approach: Language Acquisition in the Classroom*. New York, NY: Phoenix, ELT.

Richland, L., Kornell, N., and Kao, L. (2009). The Pretesting Effect: Do Unsuccessful Retrieval Attempts Enhance Learning? *Journal of Experimental Psychology: Applied*, 15(3), 243–57. Retrieved from MEDLINE with Full Text database.

Sprick, R., Garrison, M., and Howard, L. (1998). *CHAMPS: A Proactive and Positive Approach to Classroom Management*. Eugene, OR: Pacific Northwest Publishing.

Sylwester, R. (1995). *A Celebration of Neurons: An Educator's Guide to the Human Brain*. Alexandria, VA: Association for Supervision and Curriculum Instruction.

Tomlinson, C. A. (2001). *How to Differentiate Instruction in Mixed Ability Classrooms* (2nd ed.). Alexandria, VA: Association for Supervision and Curriculum Development.

Wiggins, G. and McTighe, J. (1998). *Understanding by Design.* Alexandria, VA: Association for Supervision and Curriculum Development.

Wong, H. K. and Wong, R. T. (2001). *How to be an Effective Teacher: The First Days of School.* Mountain View, CA: Harry Wong Publications.

SECTION III
CONCLUSION

Building Resiliency Is Like Broccoli

Active learning is like broccoli.
Learning is hard work. It takes time and energy to
learn. It takes brainpower, concentration, and
diligence. It takes monotonous repetition, over and
over again.
Learning resilience is like broccoli.
Active learning is like broccoli.
Even when students know that it is for their own
good, their futures and their lives, learning doesn't
get any easier. It is an investment in time and
energy. It is a sacrifice of what is wanted now, for a
better future later.
Learning resilience is like broccoli.

Actually, this was the conclusion of two researchers, Veronica Smith and LeeAnn Cardaciotto (2011). They conclude, "It appears that active learning may indeed be like broccoli: Although it is good for students intellectually, their overall impression of it may not be completely positive" (p. 58). What these two researchers did to determine this amazing truth was to look at students in large lecture classes in psychology. They worked with the lecturer and devised extended learning activities following the lecture. One half of the students participated in "Active Learning" that "required the students to reflect, evaluate, analyze, synthesize, and communicate on or about the lesson" (p. 54). The other half did "Content Review" activities that you would find at the end of a textbook chapter. What they discovered was that the active learning group performed much better in the class but was not as enthusiastic as other groups about the class. Broccoli is good for us, full of nutrients, yet young people still shy away from eating it. The truth about learning is that it takes hard work and, understandably, active learning may be perceived to be even harder work. To truly learn, a student must stick with the subject, even when it gets tough, until the learning is acquired. To truly learn, a student must take risks, fail, and try again. To truly learn, a student must accept feedback from teachers and peers who have their best interests at heart. That is resiliency.

Speaking of hard work, another researcher demonstrates that even geniuses have to work hard when it comes to learning. Dr. Carol Dweck (2010), a professor of psychology at Stanford, explains that there are two mindsets when it comes to learning: a growth mindset and a fixed mindset. Her research has led her to believe that students who have developed a growth mindset are much more capable of being resilient learners than those who harbor a fixed mindset. The students with the fixed mindset may be brilliant, but they assume that their brilliance is limited and are careful not to engage in learning behaviors that may diminish this perception of brilliance. The students with a growth mindset may be just as brilliant but are willing to take learning risks to acquire more knowledge and skills. (As a side note, the fixed mindset kind of thinking is one of the dangers of the "personality profiles" that calculate a student's color or psychological status. There is the implicit message that the profile is set and teachers and students have to deal with it, but in reality, an indication of a preference does not mean that students cannot adapt and learn to behave in different profiles.) Dr. Dweck proposes that teachers create a climate of growth mindset through reinforcement of specific growth mindset behaviors such as persistence, application of learning strategies, and level of effort. Specific praise for their behavior is much more powerful than telling students they are smart. Teachers can actually instruct students about the two mindsets and explore with them the behaviors that lead to each (see https://www.mindsetworks.com/default for more info on this). Goal setting is a growth mindset behavior that, when applied to individual student learning, can help them go for the challenging learning goals rather than the minimum. Dr. Dweck emphasizes a challenging curriculum rather than simply a successful or adequate one by providing a differentiated set of activities in order to help those brilliant students from coasting. She also suggests that simply providing students with a before and an after picture establishes that through hard work, learning growth is the result (sounds like pre- and posttests used in value-added learning).

References

Dweck, C. S. (2010). Even Geniuses Work Hard. *Educational Leadership*, *68*(1), 16. Retrieved May 6th, 2012 from https://search.ebscohost.com/login.aspx?direct=true&db=f5h&AN=53491076&site=eds-live.

Smith, C. and Cardaciotto, L. (2011). Is Active Learning Like Broccoli? Student Perceptions of Active Learning in Large Lecture Classes. Journal of The Scholarship of Teaching and Learning, *11*(1), 53–61. Retrieved May 6th, 2012 from https://search.ebscohost.com/login.aspx?direct=true&db=eric&AN=EJ915923&site=eds-live.

Section IV

Creating Communicators

Effective Vocabulary Development Is the Basis for Effective Communication

When I was an administrator in a small school district, I faced the challenge of diminishing the achievement gap in the student scores, especially in math and science. For example, we noticed that in science there was a 40-point gap between the number of Hispanic students passing the test versus the number of non-Hispanic students passing. This meant that the average of all Hispanic students' scores on the science test was 40 percentage points below the average of all non-Hispanic students' scores. Having been in the classrooms and having witnessed the teachers teaching, I knew for a fact that they were not treating the Hispanic students any differently than they were the non-Hispanic students. Also, I knew that the Hispanic students were neither more nor less intelligent than the non-Hispanic students. Even more perplexing was the fact that the school district was composed of 70 percent Hispanics and only 25 percent non-Hispanics. Of those Hispanic students, surprisingly few of them ever had been or were classified as ESL. Almost all of them spoke English fluently. So why was there an achievement gap?

The academic teams wrestled with this question for a while, but one day, when I was talking with my own children, it dawned on me what the problem was. Having been an educator for a while, I sometimes had to watch how I spoke with my own children because they would give me funny looks when I used "big" or unfamiliar words. My own children spoke English just fine, but they did not understand words like ubiquitous, soporific, loquacious, or facetious. The solution was looking me in the face. I had to ask myself, "Were the teachers teaching using 'academic' speech that the non-Hispanic students were more familiar with than the Hispanic students?"

To make a long story short, the academic teams decided to increase the level of vocabulary development, primarily using many sheltered language techniques borrowed from ESL teaching and learning concepts. The results were astounding. Because of this and an intense college-readiness focus, in two years, one school went from unacceptable to recognized and then the next year exemplary. We learned a few things in the process of increasing the vocabulary readiness of our students. Notice that I did not say that we diminished the "academic" language of the teachers. The focus was on helping students understand and speak the "academic" language. Sheltered instruction is designed with the idea of helping teachers of regular subjects accommodate for English language learners in their classroom. A close look at the strategies and the techniques of sheltered instruction will reveal that many of them are suitable for all classes. One of the foundations of sheltered instruction is "comprehensible input."

Comprehensible input, as John De Mado, a celebrated language teacher, author, and rapper,[1] would state *"is the basis of all learning."* It means that students must understand the "input" they receive in order to assimilate it into their learning. If we do anything else but not provide comprehensible input, we are wasting our time. If every student does not understand what we are trying to communicate, we are deluding ourselves when we say that we are "teaching." Comprehensible input means that a teacher must meet students where they are and provide sufficient forms of communication to make the message crystal clear. With this in mind, being a teacher really means that we help students make connections with what they know to what they are trying to know. The days of simply speaking to students are over.

Comprehensible input means that when the teacher is speaking to the students, the teacher is using multiple contextual clues that provide meaning along with the spoken words. A teacher might use the words verbally, but at the same time point to the objects being described, and then also show the words in written format. Gestures, pantomime, movement, actions, sounds, pictures, graphics, and video all are additional methods that teachers have at their disposal to increase the likelihood that their students will understand the message.

Now let's go back to my story about decreasing the performance gaps. At about the same time as we discovered sheltered language, we came across Marzano's *Building Background Knowledge* (2001), which basically establishes that before a student can grasp the concepts being taught, the student needs a mental scaffold in which to place them. Experience, first-hand or virtual, is the number one scaffold building-tool. Reading is second best, and the next best tool is intense vocabulary development prior to instruction. As a Spanish teacher, I learned early on that the mouth is connected to the brain, and if

> Comprehensible input is
> the basis of all learning.
> *John De Mado*

the mouth cannot say the word, then there is little chance that the brain will remember it. Learning new content in math or science is much like learning in a conversational Spanish class. If done right, students will leave the class fluent in the language and culture of science or they will be able to converse in the language of math. This requires that the teacher realize that students may not understand completely what reduce, simplify, analyze, compute, illustrate, or group means.

In the Mix It Up: Correlated Math and Science program from Texas State University, participants have discovered that some of the math terminology frequently means something else in science. For example, "accuracy" in math may refer to the number of decimal places of a number, but in science it may refer to the preciseness of the measuring device (i.e., grams versus milligrams). The best way I have learned to build vocabulary is beginning with a visual/verbal/aural Bloomish building-blocks method—starting easy, then getting more complex and difficult. Here are some methods:

♦ Recognition of the word in context: As I point to the endoplasmic reticulum picture on the wall, I say, "Is this an endoplasmic reticulum?" The students say in unison, "Yes." As I point to a picture of a ribosome, I say, "Is this a vacuole?" Hopefully they respond, "No." As a TPR methodology, I can ask them to stand next to or point to the mitochondria or chloroplasts.

♦ Reproduction of the words in context: After going through all of the words, I ask students to say the words, "What is this?" as I point to the nucleus. After I am satisfied they can say the words, I check their understanding, "Which organelle of the cell processes energy for the nucleus?" (mitochondria/chloroplasts) "Which parts of the cell are necessary to create proteins?" (endoplasmic reticulum, nucleus, Golgi apparatus and ribosomes).

♦ Written words in context: I then bring out the written word strips and ask students to match them with the pictures. Then and only then will I let students start reading the chapters, or workbooks, because not only are they now familiar with the concepts, but they have muscle memory of the words in their mouths and know how to say them and thus remember them.

This method is more enjoyable and more effective for students than writing the words ten times each in sentences … an all-too-typical vocabulary development technique. Possessing adequate vocabulary is fundamental to any form of communication in any discipline. Teachers must consider development of not only content vocabulary, but also process vocabulary associated

> "Writing today is not a frill for the few, but an essential skill for the many."
>
> (National Commission on Writing in America's Schools and Colleges, 2003)

with the content. College- and career-ready students not only have a burgeoning academic vocabulary, but they also have strategies to increase their vocabulary through reading and writing.

Note

1   John DeMado is an applied linguist. He is the author of several textbooks, an educational rapper and composer, and a professional developer. When I attended one of his professional development sessions I spoke with him about comprehensible input. Our conclusion was that if every teacher taught their subject as if it were a foreign language, then the main goal of math would not be calculations, but math conversations. Students would strive for communication fluency in science and students would be conversant in and about world history. Ultimately, students would learn to communicate adeptly in their own language. For more about John De Mado see http://www.demado-seminars.com/.

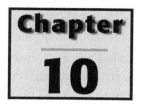

Chapter 10

Ability to Express Oneself in Writing and Orally

Communicate: Convey Meaning in Such a Way That It Is Understood

Why Do Students Need to Communicate Effectively?

College- and career-ready students must communicate effectively if they want to attend the best colleges or land the best jobs. Communication is a reflection of thinking and you cannot have the first without the last. Below we will look at how and why students need excellent written and spoken communication.

Communicating Effectively in Writing

The controversial author Norman Mailer said, "I don't know what I think until I write it down." Another famous author, Joan Didion, perhaps said it better, "I write entirely to find out what I'm thinking, what I'm looking at, what I see and what it means. What I want and what I fear." Donald Murray, a pioneer of the writing process, stated, "... all writers 'are compelled to write to see what their words tell them'" (as quoted in Stewart, 2011, p. 50).

Learning from what you write is an oft-ignored concept. Within the process of writing exists an amazing power to learn when you read what you have written. When we write to learn, we analyze, we revise, we organize, we rewrite, we evaluate, and so on until what is written is what we want to communicate. These are all higher-order thinking skills that we aspire to achieve in the classroom setting. The way it works for me is that I start with an idea and write it down. Then, if I get stuck, I play with it (sometimes like a cat with a dead mouse), I add to it, take away from it, and shift it until it makes sense to me. Sometimes I have to let it sit for a while. One of my students said she lets it "marinate." Thinking is hard work. Writing to learn is hard thinking.

The first level of writing to learn has already been discussed in the critical reading section of this book. Critical reading happens when students read the stellar works of authors and try to understand not only what was written but also the implications from what messages are being portrayed by the word choices, style, tone, and organization of the text. What better way to clarify understanding than to use writing to enhance learning! Schmoker (2006) affirms that a great way to write to learn is reading with "pen in hand," ready to jot down notes in the margins (or on a note pad if you have an aversion to writing in books), in order to capture the things we want to remember: corollary thoughts, disagreements, questions, things to look up for more research, evidence, words we do not understand, references, or more. As mentioned earlier, Cornell Notes provide a way to use writing to enhance learning and thinking. Overall, however, it is not specifically the writing that helps the learning; it is the thinking. Though writing is an active learning endeavor, not passive as in listening, the act of writing involves more of the entire body in the process and thus increases the likelihood of learning. What makes the writing to learn powerful is the process of reading, thinking, writing, rereading, and rewriting that occurs over time. Writing to learn is more than just putting words on the page for someone else to read. The focus has to be on what the writer gets out of the process of writing, not just the reader. The process of writing to learn clarifies perspectives and crystalizes jewels of personal beliefs. The final product of the writing to learn process is a summation of the thinking and learning that occurred.

Students begin to write to learn by laboriously reading what others have written and then mimicking their styles and methods in their own writing. As students get more sophisticated in their writing and learning, they will be able to reflect on their learning: what was learned, and what was not learned; how it was learned and perhaps why. On the continuum of critical writing

> The act of writing involves more of the entire body in the process and thus increases the likelihood of learning.

where you have writing for fun versus writing to learn, perhaps the ultimate writing to learn would be the point at which students arrive at reflexiveness. No, this has nothing to do with that little triangle rubber hammer tap and the knee-jerk reaction. Reflexiveness is when the students challenge their own writing and learning by asking hard questions about what they think and what they believe and how that affects their writing. Questions like: Why do I believe this? What evidence do I have that supports my belief? Does this demonstrate a personal bias? What fallacies in thinking am I succumbing to? According to Kingdon (2005), reflexivity is acknowledging the researcher's own standpoint or theoretical perspective. Yes, that is right, reflexivity is usually only learned about in the university setting of research writing, but if you think about it, research writing is the pinnacle of writing to learn.

When I first heard of reflexivity in my doctoral studies, I thought that the professor had said it wrong. "Certainly he meant reflectivity!" I thought. But as I questioned him, he explained that the research reflex action is different than a reflect action. Reflectivity only requires the writer to review what has happened and perhaps analyze it to arrive at some understanding, point of view, or course of action. Reflexivity requires the writer to reflect and then determine what effect he himself has on the thinking and writing that is taking place. This includes evaluating his own personal character, and beliefs and, in essence, includes assessing the effects of "who the writer is" on "what is being written." The idea of reflexivity also takes into account that identifying this effect on writing might be a moving target. We all have our own personal biases and preferences, and these, along with our values and perspectives, shape how we view and interpret the world. Reflexivity does not involve eradication of those things; it is simply an acknowledgement of them that may bring the writer to new insights and greater personal understanding, and which will ultimately make the writing clearer and more forceful. For example, students reading *To Kill a Mockingbird* are exposed to prejudice in a number of different forms. Reflective writing would be to put themselves in the shoes of Scout or Atticus or Boo and discover what their own responses would be. Reflexive writing would take that one step farther It would require students to identify their own sympathies, biases, and prejudices and how these affect their personal analysis of the book.

Using writing as a way to learn affixes writing firmly back into the trinity of the three R's. A 2006 panel on writing stated that writing was the most neglected curriculum.[1] How could that be? From kindergarten on, students are constantly writing. The lifeblood of schools depends on paper and pencil activities. But are those activities purposeful efforts to develop narrative, expository, and argument skills? Probably not.

How to Help Students Express Themselves in Writing and Orally

As students learn the mechanics of writing, cursively or not, the default mode of writing is always narrative. Only much later in their writing careers are students exposed to the other two forms of writing: explanatory and argument. Is it wrong to have elementary students write explanatory papers or arguments along with their narrative writing? The college-readiness standards hold that students need to be doing all three beginning even as students are learning the mechanics of writing letters and words. The College Board Standards for College Success™ for Writing are shown in Figure 10.2. As we've discussed, clarity of writing depends on clarity of thinking. The standard writing cycle is described as planning for writing, writing, and revising writing. It sounds so simple, yet why do students all over the United States have difficulty writing?

Lawrence Musgrove, an associate professor of English and foreign languages at Saint Xavier University in Chicago, had this to say about why students have trouble writing:

> When I find significant errors in student writing, I chalk it up to one of three reasons: they don't care, they don't know, or they didn't see it. And I believe that the first and last are the most frequent causes of error. In other words, when push comes to shove, I've found that *most students really do know how to write*—that is, if we can help them learn to v alue and care about what they are writing and then help them manage the time they need to compose effectively.

Figure 10.1   The College Board Standards for College Success™ in Writing

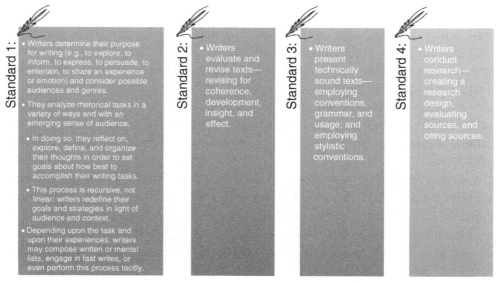

He adds that a large part of the problem with the low writing standards is that most of his colleagues would rather complain about poor writing than refuse to accept it from the students and make them do it over. He compared it to driving a car. The reasons to be a good driver are obvious, everyone knows the rules, and consequences are enforced. As a solution to the poor writing problem, he maintains that if every college teacher challenged the writing proficiency of every student, it would in essence force the rules of the road out into the open, and students would be held accountable for good writing.[2]

I would take Dr. Musgrove's interesting perspective of the poor writing problem one step further. If students really do not know how to write, the problem is not writing. The problem is that they do not know how to think, and they do not know how to use writing to help their thinking. We have plenty of tools and resources to help students learn how to write and how to think. What we are lacking many times is the will and the collective determination to help students care about good writing in every class they take. One of the best ways to help students care about good writing is to give them something to write about that interests them. This doesn't mean that students should not write about things that do not interest them. What it means is that we should provide students with strategies on how to write about things for which they do not have interest by finding an aspect of the topic that can make it interesting for them. Fortunately, we have already discussed how students can employ creativity, critical thinking, and analytical thinking to reading, and interestingly enough, these skills also apply to writing.

College-ready writers are able to write clear narratives, descriptive expository statements, and convincing arguments. But this ability does not appear all of a sudden. It actually begins in kindergarten when the teacher wrote the words down for the student until he could write them himself. The most important part of writing is the thinking that is put into the writing cycle. The planning to write, the actual wording choice, and the revising all require analytical thinking, critical thinking, and most importantly, creative thinking. As students develop their writing skills—starting with the actual mechanics of forming letters, composing words, and combining those words into sentences—certain prewriting strategies can help them engage the brain as well as their fine motor skills.

One of the best methods books for grades one through four is the *Four Square Writing Method* (Gould and Gould, 1999; 2002). The basic premise of the Four

Square Writing Method is to use a planning template made of a square cut in four parts. In the center of the square is a smaller box that holds the topic, while three of the quadrants contain paragraph detail sentences. The lower-right quadrant contains a "feeling" sentence. Completion of the template helps students plan what kinds of things should be included in a paragraph and also helps them make sure the details support the central topic. Successful completion of the Four Square Writing template gives students at least one sentence per quadrant, plus the topic sentence, for a total of five sentences. Frankly, there is no reason that the planning of paragraph writing using this method could not be extended all the way through high school. It is that straightforward and that effective. Any of the three main genres of writing work with this template.

Once the planning is done using Four Square, the outline method, or another method then the actual writing can be done. Writing more than one paragraph means that not only does each paragraph need a central theme, but there also has to be a unifying theme connecting all of the paragraphs. Tying paragraphs together requires the use of connecting words and phrases. The five-paragraph format is the basic organization technique for most writing genres. College- and career-ready students are fluent in the different genres of writing, recognizing that newspaper writing has its own organization strategy that differs from scholarly writing, just as a narrative differs from an argument. The college- and career-ready student will be able to capitalize on the similarities shared by the genres. For example, the strategy of supporting beliefs and opinions by using evidence drawn from research or personal experience is equally powerful in narratives as it is in arguments. Once the thinking and connecting of paragraphs is done, then two things can happen: the revision process or the verbal presentation of a report, of research findings, of an argument, etc. College- and career-ready students are capable of verbally presenting their ideas. Though the general structure of spoken language and written language are the same, where they differ is related to how the brain assimilates the knowledge.

Communicating Effectively Orally

In writing, the reader can go back and read what it says in order to get clarification. In oral presentations, that is not possible. Therefore, accommodations must be made to help listeners keep the main points in their working memory: fewer numbers of points, repetition of the points, and frequent review of the main points. Effective public speaking and engaging storytelling share these requirements. Speaking of working memory, as a child I loved to play the recording by Danny Kaye of the story of the animal village. This is one of those stories that is meant to be told out loud and not read. It requires listeners rather than readers because the working memory processes mentioned above are different for reading than they are for listening.

As the story is retold, all the animals are hungry, and a magic tree in the village has multitudes of all kinds of ripe fruit. But the tree will only let the fruit fall if the villagers can say the name of the tree. The problem is that none of the villagers can remember it. So they send the fastest, strongest, cleverest, and believe it or not, slowest animals one-by-one up to the top of the mountain to talk to the Chief over the Mountains. Each in turn returns to the bottom of the hill having forgotten the special name of the tree. The slowest animal was a turtle, of course, and he had a strategy for remembering the name of the tree. Over the course of the story, the name of the tree is repeated many times as each animal fails to remember it. Unbeknownst to the listeners, the repetition keeps the name of the tree in their working memory. The turtle and the listeners are able to remember the name of the tree by the end of the story because they repeated it over and over, keeping it in short-term memory and pushing it into long-term memory.[3]

Debate is another form of oral communication that is very effective in preparing students to be college-ready communicators. I have found debate to be a magnificent learning tool that engages students (sometimes too much, which is why you need to control the rules of the debate so it doesn't turn into an argument or brawl), and it helps them clarify their thinking. I know of one school district that is having great success with debates. In a blog I wrote in 2013, I had communicated with Kerri Allen, who was then the Resource Development and Communications Manager for the National Association for Urban Debate Leagues in Chicago, and she shared with me the excellent success that students in Chicago were obtaining academically because of being actively involved in the debating league (Chicago is one of 23 leagues nation-wide). These debate teams are typically composed of ethnic minorities and economically disadvantaged students, yet because of their participation in debate, they enjoyed a 90 percent high school graduation rate as compared to 70 percent for their peers, and a senior grade point average of 3.23 as compared to 2.8 for their peers (3.0 being the established predictor of college success). ACT and SAT scores were higher, and the increased vocabulary (we discussed this already), as well as the skills of supporting argument with evidence, tremendously increased the likelihood of success in college.[4]

S T R A T E G Y

Debate

A marvelous movie with Denzel Washington called *The Great Debaters* demonstrates the power of debate as an educational tool to prepare students to be college-ready communicators. Aside from showing the drama and conflict of the times, it displays the rigorous training that a debate team had to embrace in order to be prepared intellectually, to argue a point of view, to speak clearly and authoritatively, and to think critically on a moment's notice. The following are techniques that you can use in your classroom to make debate a college-readiness tool.

TECHNIQUE: HOTS debate. The typical debate format will be used: opposing sides of the same topic, limited time to present an argument and to cross-examine, opening and closing statements, etc. The additional requirement is that only the concepts can only be discuss in terms of higher-order thinking—all evidence must be provided in terms of application, analysis, synthesis, or evaluation. To help train students to do this, you may want to choose just one higher-order thinking task such as evaluation (alias critical thinking).

For more advanced groups, the arguments do not have to be polar opposites. In this scenario, two teams debate at the same time, and each team debates three times. If you have a large class and want more participation you can create four teams. You can use the four corners of the room, for example, to identify debate teams. So while team A is debating team B, team C is debating team D. Then they switch so team A debates team D and team B debates team C. In the last round, team A debates team C and team B debates team D. The arguments themselves should not be just a simple listing of facts, but should utilize the HOTS skill that was chosen. Students may find it useful to use a debate development process such as SCAN (Stop, Clarify, Ask, Now).[5]

For example, using "evaluation" as the filter, students might prepare arguments on the value of our judicial system. One side would argue the benefits and the other would present the failures. This requires students to know something about our legal system and how it works or doesn't work. It also requires students to know how to use the particular higher-order thinking skill to prepare their defense.

TECHNIQUE: Devil's advocate. This is a twist on the debate positions preparation. Instead of just supporting their own opinion and platform, students will also try their best to throw kinks into their supporting argument. So in essence, instead of just preparing one argument "pro," they also have to prepare one "contra."

TECHNIQUE: Guess my stance. In this learning activity, the teacher will have prepared position statements on various topics and have written them on stickers. The stickers are then applied to the back of each student. Each student has no idea what is written on the sticker on his or her own back but they can read the stickers on the other students. Students are not allowed to tell other students what their stickers say. Care must be taken to warn students not to subvocalize (mouth the words as they read them) as they read any other sticker. Then students must question their classmates regarding what they believe. To begin, restrict students to asking only "yes" or "no" questions. (To get things rolling faster, you can lift this restriction slightly and allow students to answer in sentences as long as none of the words on the other student's sticker are used. A student may share examples of what the other student believes.) Students will soon learn that trial and error (simply saying, "Do I believe ... ?") is not the fastest way to identify their position. Much like the only way to win in 21 questions is to identify categories first. Students first must identify the topic, and then they must ask questions to identify their stance.

If a student had a sticker on his/her back that stated, "I believe that the tenth amendment restricts the federal government's involvement in education," he might approach a fellow student and query, "Does my topic have something to do with the constitution?" [yes] "Does my topic have something to do with the Bill of Rights?" [no] "Does my topic have something to do with the amendments to the constitution?" [yes] "Does my topic have something to do with what we discussed in class yesterday?" [yes] "Is my topic about states' rights?" [yes] "Do I believe that states should control their own commerce?" [no] "Does my belief have something to do with commerce? [no] "Sovereignty?" [yes] "Education?" [yes] "Can you give me an example of what I believe about education and the tenth amendment?" [You believe that the National Assessment of Educational Progress infringes on state authority] "Do I believe that states are in charge of their own education services?" [yes and ...]. "The federal government should stay out of state education!" [Yes—you got it.]

S T R A T E G Y

Scaffold Discussions

Some students have difficulty coming up with what to say or how to start an argument. With a bit of creativity and ingenuity a teacher can start the discussions and get the arguments flowing. Below are some techniques to involve and engage even the most reticent students.

TECHNIQUE: Worst case scenario. This is another take on the debate platform preparation. To prepare to support their position, students look into the future at the worst possible thing that could happen as a result of the opposing argument. They prepare their defense from that point on.

TECHNIQUE: Partner. In preparing for discussions, some students are extremely shy and may work better with just one partner rather than a whole group. The process is the same as the four corners technique, but the debate is between two people, not the whole class.

TECHNIQUE: Four corners. An effective discussion mixer is the four corners method. The teacher displays a topic on the whiteboard/overhead/ SMART Board® and assigns a different position relative to that topic to each corner of the room. Students then choose to stand in the corner that best reflects their personal opinion on the matter. Once the corners have been chosen, the teacher gives the students five minutes to create their discussion platform for supporting their position. The debate or pseudo-debate begins with each of the four teams presenting its opening argument. Then each team has time for presenting evidence and rebuttals, followed by closing arguments.

S T R A T E G Y

Toastmasters Public Speaking

For many people, students included, standing up in front of their peers is the last thing they would like to do. But if they feel prepared and if they are passionate about what they want to say, a creative teacher can help them communicate successfully without the fear of public speaking getting in the way. Toastmasters websites have a number of aids and suggestions to reduce the fear of speaking.[6]

TECHNIQUE: Glass half empty or half full. This is a technique to help students view the different perspectives and prepare for arguments from each. Students look at their platform from a positivistic point of view and from a pessimistic point of view.

TECHNIQUE: *Magic wand*. The magic wand can eliminate the constraints of reality. In addition, the teacher can bequeath wands that have certain limitations. For example, a wand may make people under the age of 25 20 percent smarter than they were before. Students would then have to adjust their platform argument to accommodate this peculiar restriction. The restrictive wands can work with green eyes, or other student characteristics, or only those students from a particular classroom or teacher.

TECHNIQUE: *Impromptu speech practice*. Prepare in advance at least ten topic prompts per partnership. One partner will select a prompt and take one minute (you set the timer) to prepare an opening, three main points, and a summary. Then the students will have one minute to give their simple speech. Then the partners switch and the other partner takes a card and does the same thing. The partner listening is being a good audience participator—eye contact, nodding head, encouraging, etc.

Notes

1   The National Commission on Writing in America's Schools and Colleges authored a report in 2006 entitled *Writing and School Reform*, which also included an earlier report written in 2003 entitled *The Neglected "R": The Need for a Writing Revolution*. Both of these reports are foundational for every teacher and can be obtained from the College Board website at http://www.collegeboard.com/prod_downloads/writingcom/writing-school-reform-natl-comm-writing.pdf. Within the reports, you will find excellent resources and ideas for increasing writing in your classrooms.
2   Dr. Musgrove goes into more detail on the consequences such as handing out writing tickets that are attached to the grade in the class and the academic transcript. Too many tickets and the student must attend a remedial writing class or put graduation in jeopardy. See his post on "Inside Higher Ed, the Real Reason Students Can't Write," April 28th, 2006. Also read some of the comments to get a full dose of the issue at www.insidehighered.com/views/2006/04/28/musgrove.
3   Danny Kaye was a comedic actor who portrayed some of the most humorous roles in the 1940s and 1950s: The Inspector General is one of my favorites. In the vinyl record that I have listened to hundreds of times, he masterfully told *The Tale of the Name of the Tree: A Bantu Folktale*. The story can be found at (https://www.youtube.com/watch?v=eskB_ds9TAk.). For more information on Danny Kaye, go to www.pbs.org/wnet/americanmasters/episodes/danny-kaye/about-the-actor/504/.
4   Researchers from several east coast colleges completed a ten-year study (1997–2006) of over 9,000 students of the Chicago public schools. They determined that even though programs like Gear Up and Trio abound, little evidence exists to show that they increase the likelihood of college readiness. They did find one program in the Chicago public schools that does prepare students for college in dramatic ways. This is the after-school debate program. Students participating in the program must prepare arguments on agreed-upon topics and present them in a 90-minute forum where judges determine the strength and validity of their arguments as well as the style of presentation. The study compared peer groups not in debate with the debate students and the results show clearly that comparison bell curves for the debate students are all skewed to the right by at least one standard deviation. This means that debate students did better in math and reading and had better ACT scores

and general GPA than the control group. Mezuk *et al.* (2011). Impact of participating in a policy debate program on academic achievement: Evidence from the Chicago Urban Debate League. *Educational Research and Reviews, 6*(9), 622–35. Retrieved May 6th, 2012 from www.academicjournals.org/ERR.

5   You can find SCAN procedures for preparing for a debate at http://tregoed.org/teachers/about-scan.html. They also have a useful video showing how this is done.

6   You can find wonderful tips to help your students organize a successful presentation at https://www.toastmasters.org/Resources/Public-Speaking-Tips.

References

Black, T. (Producer),Washington, D. (Director). (2007). *The Great Debaters.* Harpo Films.

The College Board Standards for College Success in English Language Arts. (2006). Retrieved March 25th, 2017 from http://www.asainstitute.org/conference2008/featuredsessions/collegeboard-english-language-arts_cbscs.pdf.

The College Board English Language Arts Framework. (2007). Retrieved March 25th, 2017 from http://www.collegeboard.com/prod_downloads/about/association/academic/EnglishFramework.pdf.

Gould, J. S. and Gould, E. J. (1999). *Four Square Writing Method: A Unique Approach to Teaching Basic Writing Skills (Gr. 1–3).* Carthage, IL: Teaching & Learning Company.

Gould, J. S. and Gould, E. J. (2002). *Four Square the Total Writing Classroom: A Companion to the Four Square Writing Method (Gr. 1–4).* Carthage, IL: Teaching & Learning Company.

Mezuk, B., Bondarenko, I., Smith, S., and Tucker, E. (2011). Impact of Participating in a Policy Debate Program on Academic Achievement: Evidence from the Chicago Urban Debate League. *Educational Research and Reviews, 6*(9), 622–35. Retrieved May 6th, 2012 from http://www.academicjournals.org/ERR.

Musgrove, L. (2006). The Real Reason Students Can't Write. *Inside Higher Ed.* Retrieved June 6th, 2012 from http://www.insidehighered.com/views/2006/04/28/musgrove.

National Commission on Writing for America's Families, Schools and Colleges. (2006). *Writing and School Reform.* Retrieved March 30th, 2017 from http://www.collegeboard.com/prod_downloads/writingcom/writing-school-reform-natl-comm-writing.pdf.

National Commission on Writing for America's Families, Schools and Colleges. (2003). *The Neglected "R": The Need for a Writing Revolution.* Retrieved March 30th, 2017 from http://www.collegeboard.com/prod_downloads/writingcom/writing-school-reform-natl-comm-writing.pdf.

Schmoker, M. (2011). *Focus: Elevating the Essentials to Radically Improve Student Learning.* Alexandria, VA: Association of Supervision and Curriculum Development.

Schmoker, M. (2006). *Results Now: How We Can Achieve Unprecedented Improvements in Teaching and Learning.* Alexandria, VA: Association of Supervision and Curriculum Development.

Stewart, T. J. (2011). Aloneness and the Complicated Selves of Donald M. Murray. *Composition Studies, 39*(2), 45–60.

Chapter 11

Skilled at Information Gathering

Research: Seeking the Truth

Why Do Students Need to Be Good Researchers?

Students need to be good researchers because researching is an active learning strategy that engages all three thinking skills and forces students to be systematic and deliberate about what they say and how they say it. It expands their thinking, refines their opinions, and increases their own information literacy.

Danger of Information Literacy Isolation

Students file into the classroom and are greeted warmly by the teacher at the door. They sit down, and the teacher closes the door behind them. This activity happens daily across the United States and is cause for serious concern. Once that door closes, the students and teacher are now a completely isolated microcosm. This physical separation from the rest of the school, although worrisome, is not the most dangerous form of isolation. This chapter seeks to discuss the effects of information isolation on teacher and student scholarship, educational practice, and learning leadership.

Since the inception of public education, the compartmentalization of teaching has had significant repercussions for students and teachers alike. One of the most fundamental results has been the continual decline of teacher scholarship. Michael Schmoker, in his book *Results Now: How We Can Achieve Unprecedented Results in Teaching and Learning*, decries teacher isolation as the main culprit in slipping student and teacher performance (Schmoker, 2006). The problem is even more serious than that. Because of that isolation, teachers neglect their own personal research about how to become better teachers, symbolically closing essential pedagogical doors. The resulting intellectual isolation prohibits and discourages information literacy. The report from the American Library Association (2006) illustrates the dangers of not having appropriate knowledge of current educational research. "Information prepackaging in schools and through broadcast and print news media, in fact, encourages people to accept the opinions of others without much thought. When opinions are biased, negative, or inadequate for the needs at hand, many people are left helpless to improve the situation confronting them" (p. 7). Without solid research to guide them, educators are prone to choose educational solutions based on what the salesmen say and not what is known to be true about teaching and learning.

If a teacher and the school librarian collaborate more on the skills required in information literacy, then not only will students be better equipped to find kernels of truth in the content area, but the information literacy of the teachers will increase, too. Collaborating with librarians to improve information literacy is not without challenges in the public school arena. The same problems that K–12 public schools have with information literacy are also shared by colleges. According to Zabel,[1] "Undergraduates typically make little use of the library because their coursework does not require them to do so. This is a critical issue" (2004, p. 19). Especially in high school, but also starting early in students' academic careers, teachers must require students to do research. If teachers would take advantage of not only the abundant content knowledge available in their libraries and through electronic resources, but also the pedagogical research available, then they would be more capable of adjusting to the needs of the new types of students who walk through their doors. In addition, teachers would be able to enjoy more success in their instruction.

One way to promote active learning is not only to look at data from the United States, but also to research other countries, as suggested by Lauer and Yodanis (2004). These scholars use qualitative data from an internationally administered survey to illustrate sociological differences between countries and to increase the value and relevance of their instruction. And, more importantly, they provide a foundation of inquiry for students to discover what the data suggests about different cultures and practices across the world (Lauer and Yodanis, 2004). "Many teachers also find that the infusion of data analysis increases active learning across the curriculum" (Lauer and Yodanis, 2004, p. 305).

Becoming Teacher Leaders

This active learning is what all teachers should strive for. Teachers who regularly employs this sort of scholarly research in their instruction will also be modeling the same expected behaviors held for the students themselves. Finally, teachers must reject the traditions of isolation and become instructional leaders of their students and of their peers. In public schools and private schools, this means that these inspired teachers must actively work to establish learning communities, which are composed of small groups of their peers united in purpose. According to Rick DuFour and Robert Eaker (1998), these teacher learning teams must agree to identify specific student needs, research possible solutions, perform action research, gather data on results, and analyze them in order to be truly effective. The Wright State Teacher Leadership Program recognizes this critical need and has created a program that trains teachers to be "teacher leaders" of students and their peers. "The content embedded within the Wright State Teacher Leadership Program reflects the belief that teacher leadership is the cornerstone for both effective building leadership and classroom teaching" (Hambright and Franco, 2008, p. 17). I have established that teachers must be scholars, practitioners, and leaders in order to meet the needs of students in today's classrooms. One of the best tools they have is to be informationally literate so they never isolate themselves from professional development when they enter their classrooms and close their doors. Now how do we help the students?

Helping Students Become Informationally Literate

Because students have changed so much and every group of students has different needs, teachers must be able to adapt and adjust their instruction accordingly. As discussed earlier, this cannot be accomplished if teachers have succumbed to the negative effects of isolation. In order to combat this, teachers must collaborate with their librarians and peers on the best ways to infuse their curriculum with research skills–building activities. Teachers need to require students to do research and not only cite their sources, but also train them to choose the most trusted and reputable sources. Teachers need to help students sift through the incredible amount of information, true and false, and be able to find valid evidence to support their thinking. Teachers are obligated in this day of information overload to train students to find what is important out of all of the fluff, to identify facts, and to seek accuracy. What follows is my attempt to help you do that.

> "I have never let my schooling get in the way of my education."
> Mark Twain

How to Help Students Be Good Information Gatherers

Scholarly writing is different from other writing because of the audience who will be reading it. Accepted norms must be followed, evidence and research must be included, and ideas must flow in a logical manner to a concrete conclusion. Scholarly writing has two purposes: to increase the understanding of the reader and to increase the understanding of the author. Scholarly writing is more than simple communication. Davies (2000) makes the distinction that there are two types of writing: that which does not require composing, such as forms and surveys, and that which does, such as scholarly writing (p. 434). The purpose of scholarly writing is to lay out the facts and the evidence, organize them, and make sense of them. Scholarly writing can manifest itself in many formats, disciplines, and media, but in every case, the author establishes an opinion and offers supporting evidence in an attempt to convince others to think the same way. The stronger the evidence, the easier it is to persuade others. Gathering evidence is therefore crucial in writing strong arguments. Figure 11.1, The Texas College and Career Readiness Standards for Research, lists what students should be able to do to gather information.

One might ask how students might gain understanding from the act of scholarly writing. The mental exercise of writing serves as a tool to refine and deepen thinking. All the components of scholarly writing—investigation, building an argument, accuracy, peer review, and evidence—help achieve the purpose of making the writer think more profoundly. Admittedly, scholarly writing is difficult and requires a much higher level of cognitive activity. Davies (2000) quotes research indicating that in engaging the mental capacity to produce scholarly writing in students we might be in danger of "OVERLOADING" our student's brains, but since writing is the most important invention man has ever made to help us think, even surpassing the computer, it is worth the risk. The simple act of writing thoughts on paper raises the level of importance and trust in those thoughts; therefore, the accuracy and the quality of the writing must be increased too (Davies, 2000, p. 436). Because it is a beneficial exercise for both the reader and the writer, scholarly writing should be done more often in the classroom.

Why don't teachers use research and scholarly writing? Williams and Coles (2007) discovered that teachers say they do not use research because of lack of time and lack of availability of sources. Yet in reality, when questioned about

Figure 11.1 Texas College and Career Readiness Standards for Research

A. Formulate topic and questions.

  1. Formulate research questions.

  2. Explore a research topic.

  3. Refine research topic and devise a timeline for completing work.

B. Select information from a variety of sources.

  1. Gather relevant sources.

  2. Evaluate the validity and reliability of sources.

  3. Synthesize and organize information effectively.

C. Produce and design a document.

  1. Design and present an effective product.
  2. Use source material ethically.

their comfort level, teachers felt they were less comfortable using research because they felt they were less capable of utilizing research information than general knowledge information. In other words, they were lacking in information literacy skills. One of the first jobs of a teacher would be to help all students become information literate. Another reason that teachers may not be using research information is the perception that it is not applicable to their classroom. In fact, Miller *et al.* (2010) indicate that teachers organize their use of research into three different categories: "localized learning, easily accessible formats, and how they can apply the research to a local context" (p. 32). In reality, the only way to actually get students to base their conclusions on sound research is not to accept any conclusions that are not based on sound research. In other words, the teacher will always ask students, "Please show me the research that you have done on this topic that supports your thinking." If no research is done, then the discussion is over. The teacher instructs the student to include valid research. Likewise if the research is shoddy, or comes from Wikipedia, then the answer will be the same.

Students need to learn that the validity of the sources of the information is more important than the research itself. As educational leaders, teachers must, of course, set the example of effective research skills for their students. If we are requiring students to cite sources, and find and list references, then in the documents that we give the students, those same elements must exist. Students will need direct instruction on how to do research. If your own research skills are rusty, you can work with your librarian. If you are not an English teacher, you can ask the English department to help you train your students to perform research, validate sources, use primary and secondary sources, and use APA, MLA, or Chicago style. All the help you could want for your students to become college-ready researchers is at your fingertips. If you do a simple web search for APA format on the computer, you will see that most universities have extensive writing help pages full of helpful explanations, examples, and tips for doing research.

Student scholarly writing is so important that the College Board created a program called the Capstone Project. They noticed that students graduate high school with a jumble of disparate AP courses under their belts, and aside from similar AP strategies used in some courses, there really is no unifying thread tying them all together and making students "college-ready." The College Board provides a program to high schools called the AP | Cambridge Capstone Program and Credential, which consists of two courses taken during junior and senior years. In the junior-year course, students will learn to refine their college-readiness skills in analysis, critical thinking, and problem solving. Their senior year, students will engage in a full-blown 20-page research project. Students then graduate with an AP Credential, not just potential college credit. Both of these courses provide a unifying experience for students, an experience that serves as a capstone to the hard-learned lessons from having taken multiple AP courses.[2]

There is a growing body of evidence supporting scholarly writing in high school and its effect on preparing students to be successful in college, including vocabulary development and critical thinking skills (Schroeder, 2006; Wolsey, 2010; Peters, 2011; Jones, 2012). Because writing is an "active" learning process, it requires students to utilize all of the thinking skills: analytical, critical, and creative. It only goes to reason that the more students write, the better they get at thinking. And as I have reminded you before, thinking enhances … yes, that is right—memory!

S T R A T E G Y

Find It

TECHNIQUE: *High level searches.* Searching for information on the web can be frustrating simply because of the mountainous volume of information available at the click of a mouse. A typical search in Google Scholar will provide thousands of matches, but few of them pertain to your topic. One technique that improves the odds of finding the information your students need is not to search for the exact words they are looking for unless they already have the title of an article or book. What they need to do is back it up a level and get out of the trees. They need to look at main categories (the forest). Instead of looking for why do teeth turn yellow, look instead for dental hygiene, dental age, cosmetic dentistry, signs of dental illness, healthy mouths, diet, and dental health, etc.

TECHNIQUE: *Library search engines.* In the same fashion that looking for main categories can be helpful in finding sources, the use of multiple key terms will also be invaluable for performing successful searches. For example, if your students want information about the fall of the Berlin Wall, looking for the Berlin Wall will only frustrate them. They may get lucky but a better way to find the articles is to identify key words and terms such as what the Berlin Wall meant—separation of East and West Germany. What happened at the wall? A political and physical barrier between communism and a free market society. Why was the wall placed there? To keep the negative outside influences out of communist Germany. Key terms that can be extracted from these questions are: separation + families + Germany, political + separation + Germany, communism + protectionism + barrier, Berlin + wall + history, etc.

TECHNIQUE: *Refining the search.* One of the easiest ways to refine a search is to look at the references listed from a few of the articles that you have found. If the students find that several articles all list the same research report it signifies that the sources are valid (if three sources list the same article then you have validated by triangulating the sources) then it is a good idea to find that report and include the pertinent parts in their essay or report.

S T R A T E G Y

Sift It

TECHNIQUE: *Slice of pie data slice.* Take one day in the life of the protagonist and gather data on what is learned, accomplished, set in motion, etc. One of the most intriguing movies I have seen is called *Rosencrantz and Guildenstern Are Dead*. It takes two insignificant characters from the Shakespearian play *Hamlet* and tells their story as the play unfolds around them. In a humorous way, it also illustrates the gaps of information about purpose that these two characters experience.[3] Using their imagination, students can do a similar analysis by following the protagonist of a literary work as they perform their role in the course of a day. Students may discover reasons that the author might have left out details, or that particular details were included that would otherwise be overlooked in a typical literary analysis.

*TECHNIQUE: **Dress rehearsal**.* Students can practice the data-gathering exercise with all the actors in place. Such collaborative learning assumes that many times the answers are not available and must be arrived at through intense group interaction, conversation, debate, argument, and persuasion. Students can play their roles as if they are actually in the situation, and as a result will be able to see possible realities in the consequences as the interaction unfolds.

*TECHNIQUE: **Telling truth from falsehood, opinion from fact**.* Students need help identifying who is telling the truth, and who knows what they are talking about because of all of the information on the World Wide Web. The first thing students need to know is that just because someone listed information on a web page, it is not true. As a general rule of thumb, unless the article provides sources from reputable places, then the students should consider it an opinion piece and waste no further time on it.

S T R A T E G Y

Test It Out

Students can certainly obtain mountains of research for their scholarly writing from Internet sources, libraries, and teachers, but especially in science and math classes, it is advantageous for students to acquire their own data. They can do this by creating surveys, taking measurements, and testing hypotheses. Under your guidance, students can use this newly created data to write scholarly works of real relevance and interest to them. The following are some ideas on how this might work.

---

*TECHNIQUE: **Pilot**.* Students can perform pilot tests of their ideas. As with any "test," the data obtained from the pilot serves as the basis for scholarly writing, including argument or persuasive essays.

TECHNIQUE: Dry run. Students can walk through full implementation of their ideas before implementing them. This is similar to the "what if" scenarios often assigned to students. Being able to think through the most likely results of a hypothesis, theory, or course of action and map them out in narrative form is a valuable higher-order thinking skill.

TECHNIQUE: Simulation. Without actually performing the experiment, students will test their hypothesis as a simulated experiment. For example, the NASA.gov website is full of simulations students can use to test their hypotheses. One of the favorite simulations is the water-bottle rocket. NASA has a program in which students can manipulate variables such as size of the rocket, amount of water placed in the rocket, amount of air pressure, wind, atmospheric humidity, temperature, etc. Then students can hit the fire button and view the simulated results. Next, students can create their rocket and following the simulation, attempt to produce the same results in the field.

Notes

1 I picked out a theme from the article written by Zabel (2004), "A Reaction to Information Literacy and Higher Education," from the *Journal of Academic Librarianship*. This article was written as a response to another article discussing the theme of how to increase the information literacy of college undergraduate students. Zabel agrees with the author of the other article that the cost of information illiteracy is too great to ignore. Without information literacy, too many people are willing to accept thinly disguised marketing schemes as fact. He disagrees, however, with the other author who claims that the best way to increase information literacy in undergraduates is to require them to take an information literacy class. Zabel counters this with the arguments about the cost of college already being too high and the lack of evidence that such a course actually increases student informational literacy. Zabel also points out an alternative which is based on public school successes integrating informational literacy into core courses. He postulates that what is needed is for librarians to work with the instructors to weave information literacy into the curricula by requiring that students do actual research as a part of the course. Thus, instructors fortify their curriculum and increase the rigor and the effectual learning of each of their students.
2 As of 2017, 650 high schools nation-wide are participating in the Capstone Project. This program is supported by some heavy hitters such as MIT, Harvard, the University of Washington, Florida State University, and hundreds of other universities. You can read more about it at https://advancesinap.collegeboard.org/ap-capstone.
3 Gary Oldman, Tim Ross, and Richard Dreyfuss star in *Rosencrantz and Guildenstern Are Dead*, written and directed by Tom Stoppard in 1990. Just a warning about this film: it is much more enjoyable after studying *Hamlet* because the humor and the scenes are all dependent upon the actual play that unfolds around Rosencrantz and Guildenstern as they perform their scripted lines, and curiously react to the play in the gaps between. More information about this creative movie can be found at www.imdb.com/title/tt0100519.

References

American Library Association. (2006). *Presidential Committee on Information Literacy*. Retrieved August 4th, 2009 from http://www.ala.org/ala/mgrps/divs/acrl/publications/whitepapers/presidential.cfm (Document ID: 126315).

Azenburg, E. (Producer), Stoppard, T. (Director). (1990). *Rosencrantz and Guildenstern Are Dead* [Motion picture]. UK: Brandenburg.

Davies, A. (2000). *Making Classroom Assessment Work*. Merville, B.C.: Connections Pub.

Dufour, R. and Eaker, R. (1998). *Professional Learning Communities at Work: Best Practices for Enhancing Student Achievement*. Bloomington, IN: National Education Service.

Hambright, W. and Franco, M. (2008). Living the "Tipping Point": Concurrent Teacher Leader and Principal Preparation. *Education*, *129*(2), 267–73. Retrieved August 9th, 2009 from Research Library. (Document ID: 1803412661).

Jones, S. M. (2011). Reading and Writing Strategies for the High School Student. *Virginia English Bulletin*, *61*(2), 20–2. Retrieved May 6th, 2012 from http://search.ebscohost.com.ezproxy.apollolibrary.com/login.aspx?direct=true&db=ehh&AN=73796383&site=ehost-live.

Lauer, S. and Yodanis, C. (2004). The International Social Survey Programme (ISSP): A Tool for Teaching with an International Perspective XE "Perspective." *Teaching Sociology*, *32*(3), 304–13. Retrieved August 4th, 2009 from SocINDEX with Full Text database.

Miller, S., Drill, K., and Behrstock, E. (2010). Meeting Teachers Half Way. *Phi Delta Kappan*, *91*(7), 31. Retrieved 4th June, 2011 from http://web.ebscohost.com.ezproxy.apollolibrary.com

Peters, B. (2011). Lessons about Writing to Learn from a University-High School Partnership. *WPA: Writing Program Administration—Journal of the Council of Writing Program Administrators*, *34*(2), 59–88. Retrieved May 6th, 2012 from http://search.ebscohost.com.ezproxy.apollolibrary.com/login.aspx?direct=true&db=ehh&AN=61337084&site=ehost-live.

Schmoker, M. (2006). *Results Now: How We Can Achieve Unprecedented Improvements in Teaching and Learning*. Alexandria, VA: Association of Supervision and Curriculum Development.

Schroeder, K. (2006). Raising Writing Skills. *Education Digest*, *72*(4), 74–5. Retrieved May 6th, 2012 from http://search.ebscohost.com.ezproxy.apollolibrary.com/login.aspx?direct=true&db=a9h&AN=23254027&site=ehost-live.

Texas Higher Education Coordinating Board (2009). *Texas College and Career Readiness Standards.* Austin, TX: University Printing Services University of Texas at Austin.

Williams, D. and Coles, L. (2007). Teachers' Approaches to Finding and Using Research Evidence: An Information Literacy Perspective. *Educational Research, 49*(2), 185–206. doi:10.1080/00131880701369719.

Wolsey, T. D. (2010). Complexity in Student Writing: The Relationship between the Task and Vocabulary Uptake. *Literacy Research & Instruction, 49*(2), 194–208. doi:10.1080/19388070902947360.

Zabel, D. (2004). A Reaction to Information Literacy and Higher Education. *Journal of Academic Librarianship, 30*(1), 17–21. Retrieved August 4th, 2009 from Academic Search Complete database.

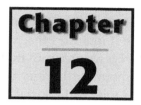

Drawing Inferences and Reaching Conclusions

To Infer and Conclude: Derive Understanding and Meaning from What Is and Is Not Stated

Why Do Students Need to Be Skilled at Drawing Inferences and Reaching Conclusions?

Students need to be able to infer and reach conclusions if they want to succeed in a career after they graduate from college. In 2016, the Society of Human Resource Management performed a survey sponsored by the American Statistical Association. The purpose of the survey was to identify the jobs that would be needed in the future (5–10 years). In the survey they used "data analysis" to not only mean analyzing the data to understand it, but to also infer what the data means by looking at patterns, trends, and outliers. Within their definition of data analysis was also the act of communicating data findings with others. They shared their findings in a report titled, *Jobs of the Future: Data Analysis Skills*. One of the major findings of this comprehensive survey is that "59% of organizations expect to increase the number of positions requiring data analysis skills over the next five years" (p. 4). The report goes on to reveal that currently 82 percent of the organizations have positions or expect to have positions from senior management to human resources that require their employees to be able to analyze, interpret, and draw conclusions from data. Another trend is that 83 percent of the organizations require their employees to have at least a bachelor's degree and of those a third need to have degrees in analytics, computer science, or statistics.

Drawing inferences has a lot to do with simply looking at words (or data). Let's look first at the word "drawing." Though the word has several different meanings, only one is most applicable to this situation. The word drawing in terms of creating a work of art with a piece of charcoal or graphite doesn't seem to fit, primarily because it includes the creation of, or fabrication of, or re-creating of something on a blank medium that was not there before. When an artist is drawing in this manner, there is the idea of interpretation and conveyance of meaning from which the artist derives certain liberties to be able to change or alter reality in order to communicate some message to the viewer. Comparatively, it is said that the best authors are able to communicate with words what artists are able to communicate with paint, charcoal, and pencil (though for the author it takes at least one thousand words [grin]). But this isn't what I would like to understand from the word drawing as in drawing inferences because that would put the artist in the same category as the writer, which are elementary roles, when in fact the act of drawing inferences lies within a much higher realm of the literate reader or art aficionado— a secondary role, more of interpretation than creation.

Another definition of "draw" refers to the act of pulling a cart with a horse or raising water out of a well. It is a transitive verb, meaning that you must draw something; the action of drawing transfers to an object, like water. If we think of the phrase, "draw water out of a well," then this form of the word draw would seem to indicate pulling something out of something else. I believe that we are getting close here. We need to look more closely at the word "infer" again. I always confuse the words infer and imply. Though they mean the same thing, one of them is used by the creator of a communication, imply, while the other is used by the receiver of that communication, infer. If the *implication* is the message that is intended to be sent, that would mean that the *inference* is the interpretation of the implication. Okay, that's it. Now we are ready for a conclusion to be made. Hmp, hmp, hmpmm (clearing one's throat) ... A college-ready reader is able to pull intended meaning from within a text, as easily and as effectively as a maiden would draw water from a well.

There you have it: a moderately succinct analysis of the meanings of the words draw, infer, and imply. The reason a college-ready reader, observer, or listener would want to draw inferences is because no author, actor, or orator writes, portrays, or says anything that does not have at least two levels of meaning. By level of meaning I refer to at least the actual meaning and the figurative meaning. It takes no great skill to interpret the actual meaning, but it takes a literate mind to be able to infer a more figurative meaning or holistic meaning. This begins with asking the question, "Why would an author write a prose in the first place?" That would be the first message that can be inferred from any text. Writing is not easy and requires significant motivation to complete. It helps to know something about the author and the environment in which the prose was written. Many times the author will intentionally or unintentionally assist the reader in this regard. Other "why" questions must follow: Why does the author use a certain style of writing? Why does the protagonist use a certain language? After asking particular questions like these, the college-ready reader will be able to begin to draw inferences from the reading as to what larger messages the author wishes to convey to the reading audience.

College- and career-ready students are able to read complex texts or data and draw inferences and conclusions by using analysis skills as discussed in chapter one, by using critical thinking skills as described in chapter two, and by using the creative thinking skills described in chapter three to put them all together to form a final message.

How to Help Students to Succeed in Drawing Inferences and Reaching Conclusions

In this chapter, I would like to model for you a possible interpretation of a piece of literature so that you can see for yourself what kind of thinking college- and career-ready students need to be prepared to do. My example is only one interpretation, but as we learned earlier, it is not enough to simply draw logical inferences. Students must also be able to substantiate their interpretations with evidence from literature.

For example, on the surface, John Steinbeck's *The Pearl* tells a story of a poor family that happens upon what some would consider significant wealth: a large pearl. Through a series of unfortunate events, the family comes to the conclusion that to find peace, the pearl must be thrown back into the sea. However, the reader can infer many other messages. Humanity is essentially selfish and greedy. Wealth is considered to bring happiness and contentment. Desperation motivates horrible acts of cruelty. Each of these inferences is exposed as if a search light was shone upon it in the different scenes of the story. The conclusion that is to be reached can only be arrived at by understanding these intermediate inferred messages and then combining them into a whole. On the surface, one might consider the story a message of futility, in which the final state of Juana and Kino was worse than the initial state. Another conclusion beckons our attention, however. A transformation has occurred. Juana and Kino began in innocence, living peacefully, but over the course of the story, their original view of friendship and their trust in humanity were altered. Then, as a response to their own reactions to the pearl, they are forced to leave behind their former life. When the trackers relentlessly follow them, their feelings of self-protection change to anger and revenge. The final return to the sea to dispose of the pearl was not an absolution of guilt, but a final turning point in the transformation from blissful ignorance of innocence to wretched wisdom of experience. The Juana and Kino standing on the beach were not the same Juana and Kino who had originally found the pearl. A possible message to be concluded from Steinbeck's writing is that life brings us pearls and sorrows, but wisdom is the final pearl.

In my Philosophy 110 critical thinking class, one of the assignments for beginning college students is to analyze a speech from a movie to help prepare to present a convincing argument. There is a great website that you will also want to consider: www.americanrhetoric.com. To show my students an example of how to do the analysis, I tried to pull up the speech from the section on movie speeches. I had originally chosen a speech labeled as one delivered by Captain Kirk of *Star Trek*. When I clicked on the link, it turned out to be only the introductory words spoken at the beginning of each episode: "Our five-year mission …." That was too simple, I thought, so I chose a speech from the movie *A Perfect Storm*. When it came time to discuss this in the lesson, that particular speech would not load due to technical difficulties. "Well," I thought, "I know that the *Star Trek* theme will load, and I might as well do a simple analysis for time's sake." So that is what I did. Figure 12.1 shows the words of the opening screens of the 1960s *Star Trek* program as the spaceship swooshes by (I never understood how that could happen in the vacuum of space, anyway).

The following are some of the questions that came up in our discussion. I was surprised that such a small text could bring out so much. Drawing inferences and reaching conclusions includes making some assumptions. A logical assumption then is that in the future depicted by *Star Trek*, man has conquered all frontiers except space. That makes me think about our current situation. If space in the future is the final frontier, what is our current frontier? What frontiers have been conquered already? What frontiers will need to be conquered to arrive at the "final frontier"? Going on to the rest of the monologue—why five years and not ten or three? What is significant about five? What is the definition of strange? To seek out new life and civilizations is a good goal, but what will happen when they are found? How do they know that no man has gone before? We thought originally that Columbus was the first to visit the Americas, but it turns out the Vikings had been there earlier. What is meant by the word man? The goal is to get students to ask these kinds of questions, to analyze the literature or text, to think about it critically, and

Figure 12.1 Analysis of the *Star Trek* Theme (Photographs courtesy of NASA Hubble Space Telescope)

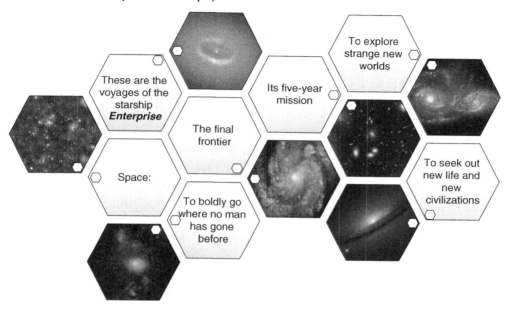

then to think creatively in order to come up with logical conclusions about the meanings that can be inferred. following are strategies and the associated techniques that can help you do this.

S T R A T E G Y

Thinking Systems

When we are "wrassling" (a Texas verb) with a problem, it helps to have a way to organize our thinking and envision the solution. Below you will find three techniques that can help.

TECHNIQUE: Issues versus problems. Problems are situations, events, or states of being that need to be solved. They simply need to be fixed. Issues, on the other hand, need to be fixed, but people do not agree on how to do it. Issues have more than one perspective for interpretation and for this reason are controversial. For example, "Students dropping out of high school" is a problem. Everyone agrees that it needs to be fixed. "High schools cause students to drop out" is a controversial issue, and there are multiple ways to interpret this statement. The very first thing students must do is to determine whether what they are considering is an issue or a problem.

TECHNIQUE: SQR4 (Survey, Question, Read, Recite, Rephrase, Review [Meyer and Kelley, 2007]). Similar to KWL, the SQR4 is a reading strategy and its variations can help students understand what they read because it is an analytical process that is ingrained into the students. It is intended for students to do the SQR4 automatically so that as they read, they go through the six steps. Survey simply means to scan the document, look at the headings, pay attention to the titles, and get a feel for where the document is going with the topic. Question refers to the act of rephrasing the subject headings as questions so that when you read, you are looking for the answers to those questions. Reciting can be done while reading paragraphs at a time (most effective), or after you have finished a section. It means what it says— use your mouth and say what you learned from what you read—i.e., the answers to the questions you just posed. Rephrase is another way of saying summarize, and review means that you look at all the notes you made while you were reading. There are several variations of this technique, but they all follow the same idea that for students to get the most out of what they read, they must they think analytically about what they read, take notes, and review those notes. Those steps are essential for improving understanding (and recall).

TECHNIQUE: Sequencing. When students are asked to write process papers about how to solve a math problem, they must use analytical thinking to determine the best sequence of events. The steps and associated explanations must follow a logical order and be replicable. However, in real life, many times we do not get to create a "how to do" process; instead, we come upon a scene and have to determine "what was done." To help students acquire this technique, a teacher can have students tell stories about photographs cut from magazines. The need for logical sequencing is developed by providing students with a final ending picture and a mix of photos of a situation, and requesting that students place the pictures in a logical order to explain what happened. A similar exercise can be done with writing. Certain stylistic elements of an essay or a narrative provide clues as to the possible sequential order. The introduction and body of a persuasive essay telegraph what comes next while the conclusion indicates what has been discussed prior. Simply jumble the paragraphs and have students decide the logical sequence of the paragraphs. This forces students to compare, contrast, and categorize each paragraph in terms of relative importance. A news article could be analyzed, recognizing that the format is entirely different; in the first paragraph are the important details, and each succeeding paragraph is either chronological or ordered by relative importance.

S T R A T E G Y

Convergent and Divergent Thinking

In terms of computer information systems, knowledge is power. Innovative companies understand that their innovators need knowledge in order to combine into new things. Even more important is the combination of knowledge from different parts of the company. Companies go to great lengths to make sure that the people in their companies have access to this knowledge. When knowledge from different disciplines is combined, it is convergent, but when new ideas and products are formed, these are divergent from the norm.[1]

TECHNIQUE: *Convergence.* In groups, students practice convergence by categorizing themes or topics from various works of literature they have read into a single unifying list. The teacher provides the topic of "finding something that was lost." Students may combine Lewis Carroll's *Alice's Adventures in Wonderland*, Frances Hodgson Burnett's *The Secret Garden*, and Walter Farley's *The Black Stallion* with Antoine de Saint-Exupéry's *The Little Prince*, all under the category of finding something that was lost. For the divergent thinking part of this exercise, students must then take parts from each story and find at least three new themes. For example, each story has elements of personal journey, each story depends on an intimately childish perspective, and each story is a story of escape.

TECHNIQUE: *Divergence.* Divergent thinking is thinking about the normal ideas ... and then what else. In a group of 30 students in any one classroom it is unlikely that all or even most of the students would be thinking in exactly the same way, yet much of a teacher's effort in the classroom is to try to get their thinking to converge. This exercise will help the students break that mold a bit. Have the students pull out their thesauruses. Have them note that each word has several synonyms. The task is to have the students write down a word that you will give them and then look it up in the thesaurus. They will then write one of the synonyms down. Then look up that word and write a synonym. This process will be repeated four or five times. As groups, compare how far each student got away from the meaning of the initial word.

TECHNIQUE: Consensus building. I can think of just a few things where a consensus is required (a jury, for example) because most things require a majority (imagine if our government had to do things by consensus, depending on your viewpoint this could be a good thing or a bad thing). This activity requires that at least one person out of every group be the contrarian— or the person who always votes against the majority. As the teacher, you give each group an issue to discuss and arrive at consensus. Using the group activity card that assigns each person a role to perform—1) Asks what do you think? 2) Can you explain more? 3) What do you propose? 4) Why do you feel that way? One person is chosen randomly to disagree all the time. The goal is to try to reach a consensus using all the powers of persuasion possible.

S T R A T E G Y

Whole Part Whole

The whole part whole strategy, or as some call it, the hamburger approach to learning, is a way of organizing learning activities so that students end with the whole, rather than just associated parts. It requires presenting students with the whole problem, then looking at that problem using analytical tools to discover the parts, and then when all the parts are identified and understood, putting the problem (hamburger) back together with some sort of application or evaluation of learning that requires integrated solutions (Mindedge, 2010). For example, "What is the math problem trying to accomplish? Can you identify the error in the calculation of this problem? Great! Now fix the error and see if the goal of the problem was reached."

TECHNIQUE: If—then and What if … Asking the questions, "If this happens, then what will the result be?" and "What if this happens, how will this change that?" is a technique that helps student understand the interconnectedness of the whole. When students start messing with the parts, there will be consequences to other parts and to the whole. Students must think analytically in order to identify the consequences and predict the outcomes. The concept of systems thinking will also help students understand that there are different outcomes for systems. Systems can be static or they can seek balance. There are growth systems and systems of decline. Dependent systems, interdependent systems, and independent systems can be described by dominoes lined up. A dependent system is one in which the dominos cannot fall unless struck by another system of dominoes. An interdependent system is similar but not only can one domino from another system begin the cascade, but one of its own dominoes can trigger other cascades in the other system. An independent system cannot be triggered by another domino but may be able to trigger other systems' dominoes.

TECHNIQUE: Finish the story. One of my projects as the gifted and talented director of a small school district was student walking tours of historical San Antonio. After the tours, students were asked to identify one element of the tour and eliminate it from San Antonio history. Then they were asked to postulate on the ripple effects that that one historical instance would or could have had on modern San Antonio, the nation, and the world. One of the sites on the tour was the Alamo. One of the groups postulated that if the Battle of the Alamo had not occurred, then Texas would have been a part of Mexico at the time of the Civil War, and therefore the large numbers of cattle that supplied the Confederate troops may not have been available. This would have altered the course of the war as well as its aftermath.

TECHNIQUE: Reverse Engineering. Similar to the reverse process paper, reverse engineering is a valuable technique for helping students identify similarities and differences. I participated with a group of ninth graders as they were given an assignment to reverse-engineer a situation in a Ford PAS class. Ford PAS stands for Partnerships for Advanced Studies and is a STEM/Business inquiry-based program, sponsored by the Ford Fund (not the Ford Foundation—different pockets of money, same company). I observed these ninth graders reverse-engineer the breaking of a clay pot with a hammer. Based on the location of the pieces on the ground after the breaking incident and the size of the pieces scattered about, the students were able to re-create the hammer's exact location of impact on the clay pot, as well as the force and angle of the impact. In order to do this, the students had to find all the pieces, graph their relative locations, use the pieces to reassemble the pot (Super Glue works best), mark the impact point on the reassembled pot, and then analyze the dispersion graph to determine angle and force of the blow. Reverse engineering can be applied to more than clay pots and computers (have you seen the movie *Paycheck* (2003) starring Ben Affleck?). Reverse engineering principles can be applied to all sorts of math problems: given a solution, determine how it was derived; chemistry problems: given a solution, determine the process to create the solution; history problems: given the gross national product, determine the economic factors that caused it; and English problems: given a Sherlock Holmes solution, determine the deductive path he used to solve the case.

Note

1 You can read about creativity and how knowledge both enhances divergent thinking and inhibits it in this interesting report. Müller-Wienbergen et al. (2011). Leaving the Beaten Tracks in Creative Work: A Design Theory for Systems That Support Convergent and Divergent Thinking. *Journal of the Association for Information Systems, 12*(11), 714–40. Retrieved March 29th, 2012 https://search.ebscohost.com/login.aspx?direct=true&db=bth&AN=71702708&site=eds-live.

References

Meyer, K. and Kelley, M. (2007). Improving Homework in Adolescents with Attention-Deficit/Hyperactivity Disorder: Self vs. Parent Monitoring of Homework Behavior and Study Skills. *Child & Family Behavior Therapy, 29*(4), 25–42. doi:10.1300/J019v29n04_02.

MindEdge. (2010). *Considering the Whole Part Whole Learning Model.* Retrieved February 29th, 2010 from http://www.mindedge.com/MindEdge_WPW_WhitePaper.pdf.

Müller-Wienbergen, F., Müller, O., Seidel, S., and Becker, J. (2011). Leaving the Beaten Tracks in Creative Work—A Design Theory for Systems that Support Convergent and Divergent Thinking. *Journal of the Association for Information Systems, 12*(11), 714–40. Retrieved March 29th, 2012 https://search.ebscohost.com/login.aspx?direct=true&db=bth&AN=71702708&site=eds-live.

Society of Human Resource Management. (2016). Jobs of the Future: Data Analysis Skills. Retrieved March 30th, 2017 from https://www.shrm.org/hr-today/trends-and-forecasting/research-and-surveys/Documents/Data-Analysis-Skills.pdf.

Steinbeck, J. (1945). *The Pearl.* New York, NY: Penguin.

Woo, J. (Producer), Woo, J. (Director). (2003). *Paycheck* [Motion picture]. USA: Dreamworks.

SECTION IV
CONCLUSION

Creating Effective Communicators

An effective communicator reaches out to his or her audience, touches their hearts, and animates their brains in writing and in the spoken word. An effective communicator creates a common understanding by choosing powerful vocabulary to convey powerful meaning. The future of our society depends on students leaving our schools as college- and career-ready communicators. Today, communication is instantaneous, and so is miscommunication. Once an electronic message has gone out, it is very difficult to retrieve it from the four corners of the Earth. Even still, technology enhances communication more than it disables it. For example, the California condor is one of the most efficient travelers. It can glide for hours with only a twitch of its tail. Students using technology gain the same kind of efficiency at communicating with a few clicks of a mouse. The bottom-line question that we need to ask is, "How can I employ all of this to help get students college- and career-ready?"

FINAL NOTES

Effective communication is dependent on knowledge gained through effective research. Effective research depends on diligent scholarship of well-trained minds. Developing these incredibly important habits of mind depends on large quantities of practice in thinking analytically, thinking critically, and thinking creatively. It is my hope that you, as a teacher, scholar, or practitioner of learning, have gained a higher vision of your calling as an educator, and that you will use this book to be able to look beyond the minimum standards imposed by the states and the federal government, and establish the ten mental habits that I shared with you as the bulwark of your instructional efforts.

1. Analytic thinkers (they think about the parts and pieces of the whole);
2. Critical thinkers (they think about effectiveness and validity of arguments);
3. Problem solvers (they synthesize disparate parts to create a solution);
4. Inquisitive (they have curiosity enough to research and discover independently);
5. Opportunistic (they take advantage of learning opportunities, and prefer to learn now rather than later);
6. Flexible (they have the ability and desire to cope with frustration and ambiguity and work with others on a team or collaboration);
7. Open-minded (they are willing to accept critical feedback from peers and supervisors or instructors);
8. Teachable (they are willing to adjust their ideas based on feedback);
9. Risk-takers (in seeking success, they are open to possible failure and ready to learn from both);
10. Expressive (they are able to communicate both in writing and orally).

The Texas College and Career Readiness Standards contains an entire chapter on the cross-curricular skills that this book discusses. Several other states have similar standards. The purpose for these college- and career-readiness standards is to guide our thinking about what to teach so we can focus more on how to teach it and how to be more effective at inspiring learning in our students.

29490510R00115

Made in the USA
Columbia, SC
22 October 2018